D1259589

Tone, Twang, and Taste

Tone, Twang, and Taste:
A Guitar Memoir

Pete Kennedy

HIGHPOINT

This edition published by Highpoint Life, an imprint of
Highpoint Executive Publishing.
For information, write to info@highpointpubs.com.

First Edition
ISBN: 978-1-64467-753-7

Library of Congress Cataloging-in-Publication Data

Kennedy, Pete
Tone, Twang, and Taste

Summary: "*Tone, Twang, and Taste: A Guitar Memoir* offers musical
and cultural observations from one of today's most accomplished and
versatile musicians, following his own career and collaborations with
some of the top performers of the past fifty years."
– Provided by publisher.

ISBN: 978-1-64467-753-7 (paperback)
Memoir: Music

Library of Congress Control Number: 2018960529

Cover and interior design by Sarah M. Clarehart
Cover photo: Pete Kennedy

10 9 8 7 6 5 4 3 2 1

Praise for Pete Kennedy

"As a musician, Pete Kennedy has been there and done that for decades, and now he's telling all the stories that have held his friends spellbound in conversation. Turns out he's as stylish a writer as he is a player. Reading him is as satisfying as hearing a great song."
— **Anthony DeCurtis, Author of *Lou Reed: A Life***

"Pete Kennedy's memoir is an entertaining, enlightening and unforgettable journey down the highways and byways of America's music scene. It's a trip you don't want to miss."
— **Peter Quinn, author, *Banished Children of Eve* (winner, American Book Award)**

"The perfect sideman who fits into any gig, and *Tone, Twang, and Taste* lays it all out."
— **Steve Addabbo, Grammy-winning producer/engineer who mixed Bob Dylan's "Another Self Portrait" and "The Cutting Edge"**

"Pete Kennedy can craft prose that stands up to his best songwriting, and that's saying something. This fine tale of hanging with the greats across the entire spectrum of contemporary music—and even being blessed by the Reverend Al Green—is a moving and deft blend of memoir and music history. A treasure."
— **Alanna Nash, author of *The Colonel: The Extraordinary Story of Colonel Tom Parker and Elvis Presley***

"Pete Kennedy is a wonderful player who is like a professor of music prowling about onstage in the guise of a folk guitarist."

— MCA/Electra recording artist Nanci Griffith

"Very good technique. I wish you a lot of success!"

— Chet Atkins

"Pete Kennedy plays and sings pretty good, and he's not a pain in the ass."

— Danny Gatton

*Dedicated to the mentors who were
generous enough to share their time
and talent with a pesky kid;
Chip Cliff, Danny Gatton, Joe Pass,
Charlie Byrd, Doc Watson,
and the best rhythm guitarist
I ever heard, Maura Kennedy.*

Contents

Prologue: Dreams

I'm a lucky guy. I'm well aware that, as we reach adulthood, the dreams that we embraced as youngsters are meant to fade, making way for the sober responsibilities of adulthood. Somehow, I seem to have skipped over that dreary rite of passage. On the exact day that I turned twelve years old, at the threshold of my teen years, The Beatles appeared on the Ed Sullivan television show. Baby boomers all over America saw an alternative to the grim enculturation of the Cold War era, the paranoid McCarthyism that groomed us to buckle down in grey office cubicles. The Beatles chucked all of that out the window. They were making music, joking around, traveling the world, and, in their easy camaraderie, they were more successful than the taskmasters who were advising us to prepare for an adulthood of lowered expectations. My dream was to emulate the rock and rollers: make music, joke around, and travel the world. My notion of success would be based on my ability to keep doing those things indefinitely.

At this point, I can rest easy in the knowledge that I got away with it. I held onto my dream and used it as a polestar to guide me down a long road. Some events and circumstances, including marrying one of the world's most beautiful and charismatic women, have been way beyond what I dreamt of as a kid, looking out the window of Saint Thomas More Parish School. I've been blessed with a surfeit of dreams that have come true, and I've managed to avoid some of the obstacles, including fame and fortune, that might have blocked my path as I kept on keepin' on to the next gig. There were indeed a lot of next gigs, but I'll start back at the beginning, under the big top...

Chapter 1: Where's Pete?

It was Saint Patrick's Day in the late 1950s. This was the single day of the year when the Kennedy kids got pulled out of school for no reason other than that the circus was in town. The whole family piled in the car and headed over to Washington Coliseum, down near the freight yards. The Flying Wallendas were walking on a wire high above the three rings when my older sister noticed I was nowhere in sight. The family mobilized for a search.

My hideout was only a few rows down in the bleachers. The circus band was set up there, playing fanfares and marches, and providing drum rolls and cymbal crashes to underscore acts of derring-do. For me, the clowns and tigers had all disappeared from view; the trumpets and trombones were all muted: a pied piper had called me down from my seat, to crouch right behind the bandstand. It was a guy with a guitar. As he strummed, I tried to imitate the easy, rolling rhythm of his right hand. Hiding in the dark, in that big, smoky boxing arena, I felt at home. It was my first guitar lesson.

I was collected by the family and duly scolded, but on the ride home, I secretly felt that I now knew something. I *knew* who I was going to be. I would be the guy with the guitar.

My older sister, Maureen, was very hip about music. She was a sock hopper. She flipped over "Rock Around the Clock," sang along with "Yakety Yak," and wept uncontrollably to "Tell Laura I Love Her." She walked home from school every afternoon through the vacant lot that connected our dead-end block with the schoolyard, and tuned in to "American Bandstand." The house rang out with rock and roll, and it was fun.

We all loved Buddy Holly, the Coasters, Duane Eddy's twangy guitar, and Elvis, who we thought of as a hilarious comedy act. I really liked Tennessee Ernie Ford singing "Sixteen Tons," with its ominous clarinet riff. The family favorites, and Maureen's heartthrobs, were Don and Phil, the Everly Brothers. My younger sister, Christine, and I spent countless happy hours jumping up and down on the upstairs couch, strumming tennis rackets as we sang along with "Bird Dog," "Problems," "Should We Tell Him," and "Wake Up Little Susie." Rock and roll was the antidote to the knuckle-rapping discipline of Catholic school in the 1950s. Subversively, those little 45 rpm records were creating a generation of rocking young rebels.

It was a big event when Maureen threw a combined twist and hula-hoop party. Christine and I were excited to hang out on the periphery of a bunch of cool, gum-chewing teens. The little RCA turntable was dropping 45s from a stack piled on the autochanger. The teens danced to "Don't Be Cruel" and "Shake, Rattle and Roll," and the girls swooned when Ricky Nelson sang "Travelin' Man."

I got on my bike and wheeled slowly around in circles in front of the house. Records were blaring from inside, kids were dancing and gorging on ice cream; it was teenage heaven. Lost in this reverie, and simply enjoying the balmy night on my bike, I was unprepared for what happened next.

A record dropped onto the turntable inside the house. Like Duane Eddy, there was no singing, but unlike Duane's deep, rumbling twang, this guitar had a keening sound, almost like someone crying. It made me happy and sad at the same time, and when the melody changed in the middle, it hit me like a thunderbolt. I found myself transfixed. It was something new, but also mysteriously familiar. It was more familiar than school, more familiar than our dead-end block or the vacant lot. This sound was like the missing piece in the puzzle of my life. I couldn't explain it. All I could do was listen to it, let it wash over me like a wave. Maybe I could make that sound myself.

I dropped my bike in the front yard. Maureen was telling everybody to listen up; the next record was a new sound. The voice started singing, "My mamma told me, you better shop around." It was a new sound, all right, but everything, for me, had a veil over it. That chord, the A minor in the bridge of "Walk, Don't Run," had changed my life. I had to find that sound again, and I had to figure out how to make it.

I was tuned in to my transistor radio all the time when I wasn't sitting in class. I hid it under my pillow at night, listening until the "Star-Spangled Banner" signaled the AM radio sign-off at midnight. I found other moments that affected me the way "Walk, Don't Run" had. There were the aching melodic beauties of "Apache," "Sleepwalk," and "Telstar." Other instrumentals, like "Midnight in Moscow" and "Washington Square" stuck in my mind, and got me through the long afternoons in school, playing the tunes in my head. There were vocal melodies that hit me, too, like "Let It Be Me" and "The Man Who Shot Liberty Valance," and there were teen pop songs like "Will You Still Love Me Tomorrow?" and "The Night Has a Thousand Eyes." Some of the songs had little moments that flashed like diamonds; the guitar solo in "Soldier Boy," or the oboe fills in "Sweet Talkin' Guy." There were country flavored songs like "The End of the World," "The Wayward Wind," and Hank Locklin's plaintive "Please Help Me, I'm Falling" that seemed to speak directly to me from the tiny speaker.

My sisters and I were never without those little radios, and we became fans of the local DJs. I liked Harv Moore, the Morning Mayor, and the Wild Man, Jack Alix, whose slogan was, "Whoa, whoa, whoa, whip it on me!"

I could take the music on my bike and ride from one melodic epiphany to the next. We soon wrested control of the car radio from my parents. One day, the whole family was riding in the car when a totally different sound came on the radio. It had a locomotive energy that grabbed me, and the words seemed to lift me up, like the hymns at Sunday Mass did sometimes. Maureen leaned over to me. "Listen to this. This is the new thing. It's protest music, and the words are important. This makes everything else out of date." As the song carried me along, I knew she was right. "It's called folk music." By the time the impassioned singers reached the climactic lines, "It's a hammer of justice, it's a bell of freedom, and it's a song about love between my brothers and my sisters, all over this land," the whole family was converted to folk music.

Peter, Paul, and Mary albums now monopolized our new LP-playing turntable in the recreation room. For a kid who loved melodies, it was a bonanza; the words seemed tied in with the excitement in the air about Martin Luther King, the brave southern preacher who was standing up to racism. When the Ku Klux Klan marched down our block to protest integration, we blasted "If I Had a Hammer" out of our windows. We weren't scared—we had these passionate voices, these driving guitars to back us up.

I felt that these people were more than entertainers like Elvis. I loved the guitar picking on "Don't Think Twice, It's All Right." They were mentoring me, leading me in a good direction, and I started carefully reading the lyrics and liner notes on the back of the albums. I noticed that someone with the folkish sounding name Bob Dylan had written a number of the songs. I pronounced the last name "Die-lan," and I wondered who he was. A wise old man, surely, to have written a stirring anthem like "Blowin' in the Wind." "Someday," I resolved, "I'm gonna find out who this Bob Die-lan is."

Maureen jumped headlong into folk music. She hung out at a radical place called "The Potter's House" in Adams Morgan, a Bohemian part of D.C. where young people sang protest songs and read poetry. Christine and I were envious of her hipness and mobility. As college beckoned, Maureen got her full folk credentials when she bought a guitar, a twenty-dollar Harmony flattop. The instrument was her entrée into the cool parties on campus, and also served as boyfriend bait. A boyfriend was duly secured by Thanksgiving break, so she brought the guitar home and left it in the basement. Christine and I, tennis-racket strumming veterans that we were, descended on it.

We had no idea how to tune the instrument or play a chord, but that didn't matter. It was a big step up from the tennis racket, and it was the sound that we heard coming out of the radio, except now we were making it. Our favorite lick was to pull a string sideways, pluck it, and then slowly bend it back to shape. Having never listened to, or even heard of the blues, we made up our own name for this sound: "the hound dog." We would make the "hound dog" whine for hours. Finally my parents, no doubt longing for a second riff, offered to send us for guitar lessons. I countered by asking for drum lessons first, which only served to strengthen their resolve. Guitar lessons it was. Christine passed, as she was enjoying Girl Scouts and other kid activities, and was satisfied with the "hound dog" lick for the moment.

As a celebratory gesture, I decided to tune the guitar to my own formula, and promptly broke the third string. Frown. A five-string guitar would never do for a serious guitar student like me. Fortunately, my mom was going shopping the very next day in the neighborhood of a magical place, Giant Music.

Giant Music was a store that sold records. Since we bought our 45s at the five-and-dime, it was wondrous to us that a store might sell only records. I knew that they also sold guitar picks—wild multicolored concoctions. I'd even bought a few at the going rate of three for a quarter, to enhance my tennis racket technique. Now I could walk in as a guitarist and ask for a string. I approached the counter.

"How may I help you, young man?"

"I'm a guitar player."

"That's great! So how may I help you?"

"I need a string for my guitar. The third skinniest one."

"That would be the G. Now, do you need a steel string or a nylon string?"

That question stumped me. "Um, what's the difference?"

The nice lady smiled. "Well now, nylon strings are much easier on the fingers."

"Great. That's what I'll take." I counted out thirty-five cents. When I got home, I realized that the new string was different from the others. It was easy to play all right, so I boldly sat down for my first lesson at Arlington Music with one very large nylon string in the middle, and five very small steel ones surrounding it.

The teacher, a patient man named Ned, showed me how to tune to the fifth fret, and sketched out some chords—G, C, D, E, A, A minor, and E minor. A lesson consisted mainly of gripping those few chords tighter and tighter until the strings didn't buzz, and then slowly playing a dreary public domain song like "The Old Grey Goose is Dead." I gathered that these songs were part of a shared trove of folklore that I had somehow missed out on. It was all less than inspiring to a nascent rock and roller. *My* folklore was The Ventures and Duane Eddy. This tutelage lasted for about three sessions, after which I started skipping lessons. After my final lesson, I poked my head into the basement repair shop, next to Ned's studio. The repairman looked like a giant to me. He motioned for me to come in, and he let me watch him work. My chin barely cleared the workbench. His name was John Duffey, and I learned later that he played mandolin in a top bluegrass group, the Country Gentlemen. They played at the Shamrock, a bar in Georgetown, not a place frequented by twelve-year olds! I got to know John better years later when he was inventing progressive bluegrass with his subsequent band, The Seldom Scene.

As far as playing went, the process seemed simple enough. Once I learned to get the guitar in tune, blowing the notes on a plastic pitch pipe, it was just a matter of listening to songs on the radio and figuring out the chords. I decided to plunge ahead on my own. I could move faster, and I wanted to assimilate this new knowledge quickly. The world might change again at any moment, and as a matter of fact, that's exactly what happened.

One morning (February 10, 1964 to be exact) I showed up at the last minute, as was my custom, to serve 6:15 a.m. mass. It was a cold, snowy pre-dawn, and I had spent the previous evening skipping homework in favor of opening birthday presents. Twelve was the birthday when you fudged a little bit and started calling yourself a teenager.

My altar-boy partner, Paul, was already in the locker room putting his vestments on over the school uniform of a white shirt, navy blue trousers, and clip-on necktie. We were good buddies. Paul was pulling the white cotton surplice over his black cassock.

"Hey man, happy birthday."

"Oh yeah, thanks." Never an early riser, I was still sleepy and cold.

"Hey, did you see The Beatles last night?"

The Beatles. In my mind, it registered as "the beetles." Bugs. That was okay. Bugs were cool.

"New cartoon?"

"Nope. They're a band, like the Beach Boys, but different. They've got long hair."

"The beetles are a band?"

"Yeah. They're gonna be on again next week, on *Ed Sullivan*."

I'd never watched *Ed Sullivan*. It was grownup stuff. Alan King, smoking a cigar, telling jokes I didn't get.

"Okay, I'll watch it."

"Oh, you'll hear them on the radio before then."

Monsignor Taylor leaned his head into the locker room and boomed imperiously, "Well, are we going to serve Mass this morning, or talk about television shows?"

We filed out into the sanctuary, muttering in Latin. I was actually a fan of the magical Latin Mass, and I loved the mysterious, stark Gregorian Chant, but my musical taste was about to go through a sea change.

I heard "She Loves You" and "I Want to Hold Your Hand" on the radio that week, and of course my sister Christine and I tuned in to the second *Ed Sullivan Show* appearance the following Sunday. A shopping trip ensued shortly thereafter, to procure stacks of Beatles trading cards, Beatles magazines, Beatles posters, a Beatles pillow, and a set of scale model Beatles that I painstakingly assembled in a haze of Testors glue. What I really wanted was an electric guitar like the ones they played, but that was still way out of reach. I started working on their songs, using my little Harmony acoustic guitar.

Once The Beatles took over teenage life, Chris and I became avid collectors of all things Liverpudlian. The real goal was to get every Beatles record that came out, and they came out in a flurry, consuming most of our allowance. Our detailed perusal of the photos and album covers revealed that they did indeed play electric guitars much of the time, switching over to acoustics for the folkier tunes. I studied a picture of John Lennon on the cover of "The Beatles' Second Album," and by copying his hand position, I found the basic Chuck Berry rock and roll lick. That, I decided, was the way forward, and that way would demand an electric guitar.

There were guitar shops in Greenwich Village, but that was far away from Arlington, Virginia. As it happened, though, my family made our annual all-summer trip to New York City, where the main cadre of relations lived. My maternal grandparents were the hub around which the rest of us revolved, and they lived for many years in a flat in the Gramercy Park Hotel. This would become a notorious rock and roll location a few years later, but in the late '50s and early '60s it was just a great place for a kid to spend the summer, located right on Gramercy Park itself. I'm sure some of my toy soldiers and dinosaurs are still hidden in the underbrush there.

In the mid '60s, this extended family migrated out of the city to New Jersey. There were many grandchildren and cousins to house, so the relations spread out around Bergen County. Nana and Pop settled in a large flat overlooking a park on Anderson

Street in Hackensack. From there, I could walk to Main Street and visit any number of record shops selling the latest 45s for seventy-five cents.

The centerpiece of Main Street was a large Sears and Roebuck store, and that's where, in June of 1965, I found my holy grail. Upstairs in the Sears appliance department was a selection of electric guitars. They were marvelous bits of design, with real lipstick tubes repurposed as pickups and small amplifiers built right into the carrying case. They were branded "Silvertone," but they were actually made by a wonderfully quirky company called Danelectro, located in Neptune, New Jersey. They were guitars from Neptune. The top-of-the-line model, a cherry sunburst sprayed with silver sparkles, and the aforementioned amp-in-case, cost around eighty dollars. I made a deal with my dad that if I got a paper route back in Virginia, and managed to save forty dollars by Christmas, he would match that amount. We put twenty dollars down on the guitar in Hackensack, with the understanding that it would be picked up at the Sears down in Arlington in December.

That launched the most exciting six months of my life. After school I would pick up my papers, hurl them from my bike in the general direction of the doorsteps on my route, and then pedal directly over to Sears. There, I could spend the afternoon practicing on the guitar that would become mine on December 25th. After a few weeks of this, the salespeople, who knew how to sell refrigerators but not guitars, would respond to any musical questions by saying, "Ask that kid over there." Thus I became an unpaid junior salesman at Sears, and I unofficially started giving my first rudimentary guitar lessons to the prospective customers.

Christmas did indeed arrive, and without further ado I opened the guitar case, plugged in, and started playing "Jingle Bells." Not singing along with chords, but actually playing the melody on the guitar. This segued into every other holiday song I could recall. My sisters gradually drifted away to start on their new Nancy Drew mysteries, and my impromptu concert turned into a solitary practice session. That day cemented an idea in my musical process that persisted for decades: that playing a song meant playing the *melody* of the song, not just chords (or later, wild rock soloing): actually play the song the way a singer would sing it. I think this was because "Walk, Don't Run" had affected me so strongly before I ever even touched an instrument. It was all about the melody.

My ear for melody served me in good stead when I joined my first band, The Vipers. At the first practice, we had to determine who could play licks from Rolling Stones records like "Satisfaction" and "The Last Time," who could play just the chords, and who could only play a few notes hither and yon. Thus we divided the three guitarists into lead, rhythm, and bass, based on our skill sets. No one had an actual bass at the time—we just used a guitar. I was the only member with an amp, so we all plugged into it. The vocal sound system was a Wollensak reel-to-reel recorder that someone had "borrowed" from the language lab at school. It had a tiny speaker, and if we put it on the ground several feet in front of the band, a listener could make out a few distorted lyrics now and then.

We played our first show in the drummer's garage. Our parents and siblings sat on folding chairs in the driveway. Curious neighborhood kids gathered around, sometimes punching each other or running madly around the yard—inspired by the tribal beat, no doubt. Our big number was "Secret Agent Man." Since the vocals were largely inaudible, the lead guitar was by default a prominent feature. I was very satisfied with that.

The Vipers worked up a number of songs, including "Gloria," "Louie Louie," "Satisfaction," "You Really Got Me," and "House of the Rising Sun." These became garage rock standards because a million bands in garages around the world were struggling to learn the same songs. Each one was a guitar lesson for me, and I began to see how patterns repeated from one song to another, getting an idea that music was something more than trying to memorize fingerings. The day when I realized that "Louie Louie" and "Get Off of My Cloud" had the same chords, only in a different key, marked the opening up of a world of possibilities.

My Silvertone was a great step forward, but I had still never seen, much less played, a really good guitar like a Fender or a Gibson, or seen a professional band play. I was really anxious to go to a rock show to witness what lay beyond the garage.

Chapter 2: Rock and Roll Riot!

In June of 1966 I decided to dive in headlong by going to a show featuring real rock stars. Since The Vipers played a number of Rolling Stones songs (they didn't overwhelm us with the lush jazz chords and un-learnable harmonies of Beatles' songs), I was excited to see that The Stones were coming to the Washington Coliseum, the boxing arena near Union Station in D.C. This was the same place where I had silently watched the circus guitar player years before. Surprisingly, my mom was more than willing to drop me off, then come back and look for me on the sidewalk a couple of hours later.

The Stones sang to the accompaniment of the screaming of five thousand female fans in the arena. Moptopped Brian Jones ignored them and played with his back to the crowd through most of the show; occasionally he'd turn around to make a lunge at the audience, which induced screaming at decibel levels heretofore unknown to man. After about a half an hour, typical length for a rock show in the day, guitarist Keith Richards plugged into his fuzz pedal and sounded the opening notes of "Satisfaction," which proved to be the closing notes of the show. About a hundred teenage girls, overcome with desire to touch and perhaps tear to pieces their idols, stormed onto the stage. The Stones unplugged their guitars and ran for their lives toward the loading dock. I don't recall if Mick Jagger even had a chance to sing the first line, "I can't get no...." It was, all in all, the perfect ending to a rock and roll show.

After that experience, my life pretty much revolved around playing in bands and anticipating whatever rock concert was on the horizon. The Stones show, like most concerts, was a three-dollar ticket. My younger sister Christine started joining me on concert trips around town. We were both still too young to drive, but our mom was more than happy to drop us off, maybe thinking we might run off with a band, giving her a couple of fewer mouths to feed!

There was one rock spectacle that couldn't be missed, and that was The Beatles. That outdid even a Rolling Stones riot. The Beatles topped the ticket price scale as well: an exorbitant five dollars!

The D.C. concert, which turned out to be about a dozen shows short of their retirement from live performance, was in a full-size stadium. Rather than drop us off, Mom had Maureen, who still loved the Everly Brothers but was not a rabid Beatles fan, chaperone us throughout the show. Chris and I still owe her one for the hazardous duty of sitting in the midst of twenty thousand screaming teens, all of them focused on four small figures down there around second base. No jumbo screens in those days, so each Beatle appeared about the size of a second baseman on the field.

We were caught up in the collective buildup of anticipation after The Ronettes, who appeared to teenage boys like three rock and roll goddesses, quit the stage. The final prep was made for the Fab Four to appear. At one point, a tall bespectacled man came up out of the dugout and strode to the stage carrying a Rickenbacker 12-string guitar in one hand and a Hofner violin-shaped bass in the other. These iconic symbols were all the assurance the crowd needed that we were actually sharing the same space on planet Earth with The Beatles. The guitars, even with no rock gods in sight yet, set off a thunderstorm of screaming that shook the foundations of the stadium.

Shortly thereafter, the four Beatles themselves emerged from the dugout and walked across the field to the stage. They each had a camera, and they were pivoting around taking photos of the crowd, anticipating (or perhaps knowing for certain) that they would soon be done with this part of their lives. Once onstage, the sound pressure level of the crowd was like a white-noise generator that went up and down in volume, but never stopped. Paul McCartney seemed the most adept at controlling the overall screaming level by jumping, twirling around, or doing the patented Beatles head shake. John Lennon was Paul's irreverent foil, goofing around. George Harrison looked straight ahead and over the high stadium walls, perhaps already focused on larger things than pop music. Ringo Starr was sequestered behind them on a high platform. I think that there have been few drummers who could power a rock band over a screaming stadium crowd with no microphones to amplify his drums. He was a powerhouse, a great drummer.

The Beatles themselves were barely audible, but that wasn't the point. The point was that in the moment of a Beatles concert, the baby boom generation came together and said, "This is *our* thing. We didn't inherit this. These guys created a new identity, a new modernism, and it's the sound, the feel, the attitude of our own generation." That's what a Beatles concert was all about.

The Beatles' show was a moment of affirmation that, guitar in hand, I was on the right track. The year 1966 was pivotal in another important way. It was the end of eight childhood years in parochial school, and the beginning of my teenage years in high school. That meant a new circle of friends. I joined another band, The Figments of Imagination. We had all come up through the garage band scene, and we were ready to learn a broader range of songs. Beatles songs were now considered approachable, and the harmonies of The Bee Gees and The Hollies were something that could be worked up with effort. Something called a "rave-up" was introduced by The Yardbirds and their ace guitarist, Jeff Beck. It was an improvised section dropped into a rock song, resembling a little bit of free jazz. A rave-up focused the attention away from the singer, and onto the lead guitarist, who would display improvisatory skill and technique. I was all for it! Rock and roll seemed like a roller-coaster ride of continual surprises.

The Figments started out as a little boys club, playing in our family's basements, but as freshman year progressed and our social circle widened, we started playing real gigs, in other families' basements! The summer of 1967 brought great music on the radio, with lots of new songs to learn as a group, and we expanded our gig circuit further to include local pool parties, where I learned to crank up the reverb for surf tunes. By the beginning of sophomore year in the fall of 1967, we were playing some high school dances and soaking up the sounds we heard and saw weekly on *Shindig* and *Hullabaloo*, the rock and roll TV shows.

On a crisp mid-September afternoon of that year, Mom dropped Christine and me off on Constitution Avenue, near the Washington Monument. Tourists milled about, squinting at their maps, befuddled by the layout of traffic circles and slanting avenues. L'Enfant designed the city to confuse British troops in case of an invasion, and the Byzantine layout has worked equally well for invading tourists. As a matter of fact, the British *were* invading Washington that day, and Chris and I were holding tickets. We made our way into Constitution Hall and found our seats in the box just above stage right. It was mid-afternoon, but the big hall was deliciously dark when the house lights went down.

The first act was the Blues Magoos, psychedelic popsters from New York. They had a full backline of the new Sunn amps, and, strangely, they all seemed to be wearing scuba-style wetsuits. They blasted out their one hit, "We Ain't Got Nothin' Yet," with a concise little solo that had the basic fingerings for rock and roll lead guitar condensed into a ten-second primer.

The Blues Magoos had a couple of surprises up the sleeves of their wetsuits. At one point, the whole stage went dark, and a powerful strobe light turned the band members into slow motion Charlie Chaplins. It was the first time most of us had seen a strobe, and a collective gasp went up. A few minutes later, they delivered their visual *coup de grace*. The stage went dark again, and this time their wetsuits were lit up with flashing, crawling kingsnakes of neon. The suits were woven with electric lights! They must have been plugged in, somehow, and each guy was a one-man, gyrating light show. They were an overwhelming visual for a bunch of micro-teens, but the best was yet to come.

Christine and I went to get popcorn, and while we were counting out our change, the explosion came. A rumbling sound, like a volcano, enveloped the venerable old hall, shaking the powdered-wig portraits on the hallowed walls. We hurried back into the dark main room. Chaos had erupted onstage. The bass player stood to our left, unmoving, but his huge amps were roaring like an express train. The singer, dressed in red brocade, and looking like a character out of Dickens, was swinging his microphone in wide loops over the crowd. The drummer was berserk; playing wild fills that sounded like a rock and roll "Night on Bald Mountain." Everything seemed about to tip over, and the old hall felt like it was shifting on its foundations.

Wild as the whole scene was, all eyes were glued on the guitarist. A gangly marionette pulled by invisible strings, he was kinetic energy personified. He stared straight ahead, not acknowledging the screaming crowd, and spun his right arm in huge pinwheels. It seemed impossible that the ferocious groove that was rocking the building could be coming from this Punch and Judy team of guitar and drums, who seemed to be flailing randomly at their unfortunate instruments.

The guitar thrasher, who was impossibly tall and thin, wore tails made from the British Union Jack. He was playing a Rickenbacker twelve-string, but not in the chiming style of The Beatles. The sound was more of a crunch than a chime. Two minutes into the show, the amps were ready to blow up, and he just kept flailing. They were singing a lurching song called "Can't Explain." At the end, which was more of a collapse than a definitive ending, the guitarist hacked out the intro to "Substitute" and the locomotive started up again. Each song segued into the next, with no ingratiating patter in-between. "The Kids are Alright," into "Happy Jack," into "Pictures of Lily," into a strange, menacing "Boris the Spider." They took a moment to catch their breath, and the guitarist spoke to the crowd while he strapped on a Gibson double-necked SG. "This is a bit of a mini-opera. It's called 'A Quick One While He's Away.'" Chaos erupted again, and as the opera lurched to a halt, they roared into "I Can See For Miles." While that was collapsing into the final chord, the guitarist handed off his double-neck and picked up a cheap, student model Fender Musicmaster, the sacrificial victim *du jour*. With no formal count-off, they lashed into "My Generation," the bass solo sounding like a volley of mortar fire. The song dissolved into a crazed drum solo, and that in turn devolved into the maniacal drummer kicking the drums all over the stage, while the singer threw the microphone out into the crowd, and the guitarist tossed his hapless Fender up into the air, catching it a couple of times, and then missing it. It crashed to the floor in a blast of atonal feedback. He picked it up by the headstock and began wood chopping the stage with the body until the neck broke in two. By this time, roadies had thrown smoke bombs on stage, making it hard to pick out details in the firefight. It was Dante meets Hieronymus Bosch, and if any of the esteemed Daughters of the American Revolution (who owned the hall) were present, they were undoubtedly swooning and in need of smelling salts. It was chaos, and it was the first time the kids of D.C. heard (and saw) rock music, as opposed to rock and roll.

We had seen The Who, and they were prying open the Pandora's box of rock all across America. They weren't even the main act. After the smoke cleared, and the roadies swept up pieces of guitars, drums, and amps, the headliners came on. "Mrs. Brown, You've got a Lovely Daughter," "I'm Henry the Eighth I Am." The girls screamed for Herman and his merry band of Hermits, but the rockers all rolled their eyes. Last year, we might have thought they were cool, but now we had seen The Who, and they were talkin' 'bout *our* generation. Christine and I met Mom outside with our hearts pounding.

My band continued calling ourselves the Figments of Imagination until around 1968, when the rise of the hippie subculture, which we could only view from afar by studying album covers, required that we come up with a more intellectual name. For some reason, we deemed that "The Flying Hospital" would satisfy that need. I painted it in bold psychedelic-style lettering on our bass drum head, and, seeking authenticity, we started studying Memphis soul records in earnest. Our secret weapon was a teenage soul shouter who simply went by "Louie." He could do the patented "Wilson Pickett scream" like no one else at O'Connell High, and we started getting gigs at "boy girl parties," with mom and dad chaperones, in the local area.

One rainy Saturday, the band members sat cross-legged in a circle on the floor of Louie's front room, a tribe of garage rockers excluded from the legit school band, trying to collectively push ourselves to the next musical level, which seemed to demand a change in lifestyle as well. Pieces were starting to fit together, but there were still a lot of secrets to be uncovered. Just who were The Cream, a band you could read about in magazines, but couldn't hear on the radio? And who on earth were the Grateful Dead? Strangest of all, who was Jimi Hendrix, the wild man who played the guitar with his teeth, in front of amps so large that they formed a wall? We had to find answers to these questions. It was crucial to the survival of the band. Louie and I volunteered to venture out of the safety of the suburbs, into the heart of D.C.'s hip territory, Georgetown.

Pooling our allowances for bus fare, we rode down Route 50, past St. Thomas More, past Fort Myer, past Arlington National

Cemetery, past the Iwo Jima statue, and beyond the comfort of our paper routes and bicycle back roads. We were looking for initiation, but we didn't know in what form it might come. We got off the bus at the corner of Wisconsin Avenue and M Street, and spent the day walking.

Louie and I were the Lewis and Clark of the band, mapping out unknown territory. Hopefully, we would bring back some sacred artifact that would inject this alternative reality into our suburban wasteland. That artifact appeared in a little black-lit record shop. Louie found it.

"Hey, look at this! It's a single by that wild guy, the guy who plays with his teeth!" We turned it over carefully, as if we'd never seen a 45 before. On one side, it read "Purple Haze," and on the other, "The Wind Cries Mary." The sleeve looked like a still from a sci-fi movie. Who was this guy with his two Raggedy Andy cohorts? We had to hear their music.

Louie and I counted our remaining resources. We each had a single dollar. If we spent seventy-five cents on the record, and fifty cents each for bus fare, we'd have a twenty-five cent slush fund. We flipped the last quarter for first possession of the jointly owned 45, and Louie won. I got off the bus first. I walked the rest of the way home and picked up my Silvertone, looking for a lick or a chord change that would somehow tie together all the new things I had seen and heard that day. I was lost in the zone when the phone rang. It was Louie, and he was screaming.

"Oh my god! Oh my god! Oh my god!" That much was intelligible, interspersed with the tongue speech of a snake-handling preacher, the insensate shouting of a sanctified sister, and the awkward, absurd murmuring of a Mongolian shaman in the throes of ecstasy. In other words, Louie was excited. "You've got to hear this! You won't believe it!" He repeated this so many times that I resigned myself to the fact that I would probably never hear whatever it was that I was supposed to hear. He finally regained enough composure to put the needle down at the beginning of the record.

I heard the familiar crackling of a 45, the last jumping off point before a long journey, a lifelong journey. It was followed by the crunch of the mighty double tritone intro to "Purple Haze." Bb and E at the same time, repeated over and over. It was shocking. It was everything that had been considered wrong, suddenly made right. As the song progressed, every sound was new. Nothing was familiar. Each note seemed to blow away everything that had come before.

When confronted with something that turns the world upside down, there's little else to do but laugh. So I laughed, and by the time Louie hung up, I was energized on a whole different level. There was more to music than I had ever guessed.

The following week, I skipped all of my after-school trips to Jack's Deli so I would have five bucks to buy the full Hendrix LP, "Are You Experienced?" I studied the cover photo and graphics for a long time before I put the needle down. That same album jacket went up on my wall for years.

We auditioned the "Are You Experienced" album as a band at our next Flying Hospital rehearsal. Louie and I, the initiates who had made the hero's journey into Georgetown and come back with this talisman, acted as the high priests. "This," we declaimed, "is what we're going to sound like from now on." Jack, the bass player, took it in stride. In fact, the bass lines were playable for someone who had been listening to Memphis soul and James Brown. The drums were a different thing entirely. Mitch Mitchell was writing a new rulebook, one with no rules. When we got to "Fire," with its hyper-speed version of complex funk, Neil, our drummer, buried his head in his hands. He finally spoke. "Guys," he was choked up, "I'm gonna have to quit the band."

I knew how he felt. After all, this album signaled a lifetime of learning ahead. Hendrix had written a new testament on my own instrument, and I could either quit now, or try to absorb it and make it my own, and it wasn't going to be like learning "Satisfaction." We knew instinctively that Neil's agony wasn't just about drumming. It was about the band. For the first time, something had come along that could draw a line through the brotherhood. We couldn't let Neil back down, so we stood as a tribe around the drums.

"No, man, you can't quit. We've all gotta learn this stuff, and we'll do it together. We're gonna have to go from being a good band to being beginners again, but that's okay, isn't it? We don't expect you to nail this stuff right away!"

I spoke up, "Do you think I'm gonna learn these guitar parts by next practice?" We all fell down laughing at the absurdity of it all. Just when we thought we had something together, just when we had "Midnight Hour" pretty happening, the world turned on its head again. The phrasing of "Purple Haze" was like that of "Walkin' the Dog," but blasted into the stratosphere on a Stratocaster. But we were just kids. We were learning stuff all the time. This was just a bigger challenge, way bigger than we had ever foreseen.

Neil picked up his sticks, and Louie counted off the intro to "Purple Haze." We were on our way. As we learned more complex songs, it occurred to us that it might be important if everyone in the band could actually play well, so we shuffled members over time. We reached a high point with the addition of Tom Principato, a local high school student who had a collection of blues records and could play some real licks. We were becoming aware that blues was the foundation of rock music. That lent a special status to certain rockers, including Jeff Beck, who had ignited those "rave-ups" with the Yardbirds. He was striking out now on his own with the aid of a rooster-haired singer from the gritty English midlands. This was an aggregation I definitely wanted to see live.

It was two o'clock on an autumn Saturday afternoon, and I was ostensibly raking the leaves, when my friend Jack's metal flake green Camaro came roaring down the block, with Jack leaning out the driver's window like a hot rod Paul Revere.

"Hey man, jump in. Jeff Beck's playing at the roller rink at three o'clock!"

I couldn't believe my ears. We'd bought a copy of Beck's first solo album, "Truth," for the band to check out. The album was saturated in tangy, twisted improvisation that sounded like nobody else. The guitar riffs bounced like Silly Putty off the equally nutty phrases of his lead singer, a journeyman rocker named Rod Stewart, who was previously unknown stateside. That these guys were down the road at the Alexandria Roller Rink was too good to be true. I dropped the rake and jumped into Jack's Camaro.

When the merry lads hit the stage, they sported haircuts—rooster-comb shags—the likes of which were unknown in Alexandria. They were cool before they struck a note, but they upped the ante immediately when Beck hit the opening growl of "Let Me Love You." Ronnie Wood, playing a Telecaster bass through a Marshall amp, generated a crunching, distorted bottom that perfectly matched the insinuating sneer of Beck's Les Paul guitar. Nicky Hopkins on a chipboard Wurlitzer electric piano and Mick Waller on drums lent the perfect unobtrusive support. Beck's and Wood's flash and charisma emanated out over the hardwood rink, but they were quickly upstaged by the weird apparition who leaped out from behind Beck's Marshall amp.

Legend has it that Rod Stewart was so shy that he sang from behind the amp stacks, but don't believe it. He lunged toward the front of the stage, wielding the microphone sideways, stand and all, like a mine detector, with the heavy base upended. His sudden, off-kilter entrance disoriented the crowd, and his hair, an exaggerated version of Ronnie Wood's rooster, gave the impression of a super-confident alien taking control of the stage.

Stewart's voice sounded like he gargled with razor blades. We had no reference point to categorize the sound. It was rock singing, like Beck's guitar was rock guitar, and with a similarly raunchy tone. Stewart and Beck's voice and guitar sounded like a fight between two scabrous alley cats.

They ran down the whole "Truth" album, counting off each song out of the applause, with no wasted words of introduction. They wound up with a blistering "Beck's Boogie," during which the simple Les Paul/Marshall rig conjured cats, dogs, hot rods, jets, schoolgirls jumping rope, and even the crazy sci-fi licks of 1950's electric guitar pioneer Les Paul himself. Beck had his own electric guitar voice. He was funny, always coming out of left field, and the band was rock solid in its loose groove. They smoked.

Jack dropped me off back at the front yard. I finished off the leaves in high gear, pumped up and dreaming of Marshalls, Les Pauls, and wah-wahs, and pondering the fact that the British rockers seemed driven by a mad desire to be really good.

Once you've seen The Beatles, The Stones, The Who, and Jeff Beck, who's left? I'll tell you who's left: Hendrix! He didn't play the roller rink. He was a rung or two up the ladder, playing at the Washington Hilton Hotel Ballroom. This stage was normally used by tuxedo-clad dance bands playing "Tea for Two," but Hendrix had a mighty wall of amps erected, as did his bassist Noel Redding. Between them was Mitch Mitchell, who didn't project a crazy man image like The Who's Keith Moon, or a good time grooving image like Ringo. He was a virtuoso drummer, and he conversed with Hendrix's guitar. It was beyond just playing music. It was communication on a high level. Hendrix was electric. By that, I don't mean that he simply played electric guitar or created musical effects using electrical devices. What I mean is that when he walked out onstage, he gave off an overwhelming sense of electricity, an aura, before he even played a note. It was the feeling you get when you're in the room with an authentic genius. It may only happen once or twice in your life, even if you're lucky, but there is nothing quite like it. Of course Hendrix played great, and every guitarist in the audience (rumor has it that the legendary Roy Buchanan was there) went home with a mother lode of inspiration. I didn't feel discouraged in the face of Hendrix's futuristic talent. Quite the opposite, I felt like I was being pulled in a good direction, immersing myself in something that was truly great.

By the time I turned sixteen, I had seen a lot of great musicians, had played some real gigs, and I'd even stood nearby on a chilly autumn night while the Fugs and Allen Ginsberg tried to levitate the Pentagon with Sanskrit chanting. I had also hitchhiked halfway across the USA. That trip, the true end of boyhood innocence, was inspired by reading and taking to heart Woody Guthrie's anthemic hobo journal, "Bound for Glory."

At sixteen, my neighborhood buddy Dean and I hit the road wearing light jackets, hitchhiking with ten dollars each in our pockets, staying in communes or sleeping in the woods and open fields, all in search of the muse of the road. It was a cold November in the East, and even colder when we reached the Midwest. We were momentarily thankful to be picked up by the Kansas Highway Patrol after a freezing night spent tending a campfire in the woods somewhere west of Topeka.

We were quickly identified as the first longhaired rockers to venture into the state, and the police put their heads together to come up with a charge against us. They settled on vagrancy and we were driven to the big-city jail. We were incarcerated in a cell with actual hardened criminals who had done things besides just having long hair. That was not a good experience, and I was grateful when, a few days later, the warden transferred me to solitary confinement. You know it's bad when you're glad to be put in solitary! Eventually my dad showed up and got me out, free of an arrest record, since long hair wasn't an actual crime on the books. Flying home over the territory I had traversed by thumb, I looked down at the patchwork fields and felt road weary. Sixteen years old is too young to feel that way, but I had seen and done things that no one at O'Connell High School, student or Christian Brother, had experienced. I felt alone in the world, and I just wanted to disappear for a while into my room.

I settled back into student life in Arlington, came under the spell of Dylan, whose name I could now pronounce, and rekindled my interest in acoustic guitar when I picked up a nice Gibson J-45 at National Pawnbrokers.

For several months after I got back from hitchhiking, I lived as a virtual hermit at home, reading and staying very quiet, until my dad talked me into going to hear the folk mass group at Saint Thomas More. I was reluctant. Saint Thomas More, to me, evoked memories of nuns dispensing corporal punishment, and I'm sure my terror of it, and a native Irish sense of rebellion, had led to my teenage nihilism about everything except guitar. I didn't want to plunge back into that stiffly religious world, but when I finally got dragged to folk mass, I was amazed to find that I liked it!

The folk mass group was really good, and the first song I heard them sing was by the cool Richard Farina, so I felt like I was among kindred spirits. I went to a rehearsal with the group, and I found that, just like in the garage band days, everyone else strictly played chords and sang, leaving me to play lead guitar.

The group members liked to have parties, and they were in no way prudish teetotalers or pushy religious zealots. They drew me out of my post-runaway feeling of loneliness. Their apartments were lined with good books on homemade shelves. They liked to drink a glass of wine, listen to Dylan's "Highway 61 Revisited," and talk about philosophy and politics. In a word, they were smart. They also backed up their talk with action that seemed to me more meaningful than hitchhiking around. The Catholic Church at the time, at least the younger generation cadre, was concerned with three things: relieving poverty, critically examining the war in Vietnam, and struggling for racial equality. I could share their passion about these things. When Martin Luther King was killed, and the flames of D.C. burning could be seen from the hills in Arlington, I was glad to take part in loading food and clothing into trucks that crossed through the military checkpoints along the Potomac. It was amazing to me that, instead of rocking out at a teen dance, I was involved in a church-sponsored relief effort, but it was a good feeling, to be helping others.

The folk mass crowd, at parties, frequently played a recently issued album entitled "Music from Big Pink." It was a mysterious record, cryptic in its lyrics and in its vague back story. The group had some connection with Dylan. The evidence thereof was that he had co-written a couple of the songs on the album. He didn't do that with just anybody. Dylan's activities during a period of retirement from performing were shrouded in a fog of rumor. This group simply called themselves The Band. It wasn't until their second album came out that they started to coalesce in my mind as a real group. They wrote songs apart from Dylan and they were going to come out of hiding to tour. I was one of the first to get tickets when their D.C. gig was announced. I was enthralled with their music because it seemed to incorporate so much about America. There was folk, blues, soul, country, rockabilly, jazz, and classical all blended to a rough-hewn perfection.

I decided that night to get back into playing electric guitar, but on newly defined terms. I wanted to explore roots music further, and I wanted to play songs with lyrical subtlety. I was through bashing and crashing, and I felt like a new world of music, American music, was opening up. My friends in the folk mass group introduced me to a local band that had a rehearsal house out in the Virginia countryside. They were guys who also wanted to write songs that emulated The Band, and they sought to explore in a deeper way the common roots of folk, country, and rock and roll. That's how I came to play with Marlow Mays and Natural Bridge.

We were practicing one midsummer night at the Natural Bridge band house, working up a Buck Owens tune, when a buddy of some of the guys dropped in. He was up from Richmond, where he played in a band known as Mercy Flight. I didn't know anything about the Richmond scene, but I gathered they were a top act, and that this guy had come north with some important news.

"Guys," the emissary from Richmond intoned, "there's a cool show coming up at the end of the summer. We got the top floor of a parking garage on 7th Street, down near the VCU campus. We're gonna build a stage, and we've got the best sound system in town lined up. It's gonna be far out."

"Light show?"

"Don't need it. It's all gonna happen during the day. Mercy Flight's gonna play, and these guys from Jersey are headlining."

"Wait a minute! Some guys from Jersey are headlining over you?"

"They're called Steel Mill. They're big on the VCU campus. They're gonna draw, I assure you. Anyway, we want you guys to open the show."

"Open for Mercy Flight? Right on, brother." Paul, as the roadie, spoke for the entire band.

It was all academic to me, literally. I would be leaving a week after the show for college in Boston, so I wasn't thinking in terms of big breaks for the band anymore, but they all seemed genuinely excited about opening for Mercy Flight, so I jumped on board.

We did indeed do the Richmond gig on the top floor of a parking garage at 7th and Marshall Streets. To my surprise, the posters scattered about had us listed as "Marlow Mays and The Stingers Blues Band." I guess Marlow was covering all bases, since blues-rock was a popular trend at the time, and country-rock was known only to a small cognoscenti. Nonetheless, we played a set of low volume country tunes, in dynamic contrast to the two following bands, both of which were really hard rocking.

Mercy Flight were the local favorites, and Steel Mill delivered a hard driving set. Their skinny front man, Bruce Springsteen, had a shoulder-length mop of unruly hair, wore torn cutoff jeans, and handled the extended Les Paul solos through a Marshall amp, with a little bit of singing here and there.

Steel Mill was still onstage when the weather started looking grim. I loaded my guitar and amp in the VW, cranked up Creedence Clearwater on the 8-track, and bade farewell for the time being to Virginia, and to my childhood. The '60s were over, and in a couple of days I would head north to Boston and beyond.

Chapter 3: *The Basement Boys*

My mom, being a top-flight guidance counselor, always thought that I should go to a small, alternative college. That was excellent advice, but it went unheeded. I wanted to be in a happening music scene, and most of the little alternative schools were tucked away in the bucolic hills of dairy-farming country. For me, it was New York or Boston. New York I knew well from childhood, and from subscribing to *The Village Voice* throughout my high school years. But I knew college wouldn't be anything like summers frolicking in Gramercy Park. Boston, on the other hand, just seemed like "college" and I knew it was a hub of folk and rock and roll. With Les Paul in hand, and a 50-watt Marshall amp in the backseat of my VW, I headed north, across the Tappan Zee and up the shady lanes of the Merritt Parkway. I bypassed the city that never sleeps and headed for the city that never stops studying.

Boston College was wild and wooly in the late days of the Vietnam War. The graduating class of the previous year never actually graduated because they were on strike. It didn't take long to find the hip radio station and the hip alternative press, *The Phoenix*. That was where I learned what the cool venues were, and I vowed to hear as much music as I could.

I pulled up in front of the hall where registration was going on, and got my class assignments. No room assignment, though. It took some hiking around campus to find the room assigner, a Jesuit with a Red Sox cap adorning his tonsured head. "Kennedy, eh?" His eyes twinkled. "You must be one of the ones in Welch

Hall." I wondered how "the ones" in Welch Hall got chosen for that special honor, but I was too tired for small talk. I headed over to the dorm.

Something was odd. I canvassed the first floor, looking for room number 12. All the rooms on the floor were three digits: 100, 101, etc. I checked the basement. There were nothing but utility rooms down there: a kitchen, a couple of storage rooms, and a chapel. Apparently the Jesuits had once lived in these dank depths, or else they had designated the area as a bomb shelter back in the fun-filled 1950s. Anyway, it was desolate, but after scouring the rest of the building, I made one last trip down to the catacombs. This time I noticed that the kitchen door had a number on it: 12. I pushed it open gingerly, and, sure enough, two college student types were busily hanging Pink Floyd and Lord of the Rings posters. These were Joe and Keith, my roommates for the next nine months.

Joe was a very studious type, one of those people who seem to really enjoy life while still managing to get perfect grades. Joe also had good taste in music, and, as successive *Rolling Stone* issues announced the deaths of Joplin and Hendrix, and as John Lennon slipped loose from his Beatles moorings, Joe developed a theory that the 1970s were not going to be a landmark decade in pop music. How right he was.

Keith was not studious, unless you count weightlifting. He was an early riser, who was up and out to the gym before dawn every day. He'd stay there until after sundown (which is mid-afternoon in the dead of a Boston winter) and then, after a nourishing meal in the dining hall, he'd return to Room 12 and strap on a pair of massive headphones. He liked to listen loud; the headphones, even when attached to his cranium, were as loud in the room as a pair of bookshelf speakers. For the nine months we lived together in the kitchen, he alternated between two LPs: The Moody Blues "To Our Children's Children's Children," and King Crimson's "In the Court of the Crimson King." On the menacing hook line of the latter title track, Keith would jack the volume to eleven, bathing the room in gothic style flat-five chords. Good fun for Keith, somewhat torturous for Joe and me.

A few weeks into the semester, I was paging through *The Phoenix* when an ad caught my eye. It read, "Tonight, one night only, The Byrds at the Boston Tea Party." One fifteen-minute streetcar ride later, I was in the shadow of the Fenway Park scoreboard, looking for the club. The place was appropriately dark and dank, and sans chairs. The crowd packed in tightly, and I slowly excused my way over to stage right, in the first row of standees. The trick was to stand where I could see lead guitarist Clarence White as clearly as possible, but still refer over to frontman Roger McGuinn when his jangling 12-string came to the fore.

Suddenly, Clarence was onstage, standing less than ten feet in front of me. Roger loped onto stage left and tore into the intro to "So You Want to be a Rock 'n' Roll Star."

The high points of the show occurred every time Clarence played a solo. He rarely made reference to parts from the records, improvising it all as he went along. He was more like a jazz player, but his approach and his visual impact transcended any category. It almost seemed like an act of generosity that he was playing rock at all. His presence was like a concert violinist playing Bach. He didn't jump around like Hendrix, but he commanded the stage, wearing a long cape that made him look like a medieval chevalier. "Eight Miles High" was awesome, in the true sense of the word, and his overall carriage, one of rocking dignity, was something really inspiring. Three years later, a drunk driver would kill Clarence. I didn't know it, but I was lucky to be standing in that dark club, so far away from home, but feeling so at home in the world of guitar.

A few weeks after the Byrds show, I saw another ad in *The Phoenix*, for another one-nighter. This time it was the Duke Ellington Orchestra at the Jazz Workshop. I thought of Duke as a demi-god who inhabited the Valhallas of Lincoln Center and

Carnegie Hall. I couldn't believe he was playing at a small club. In five minutes, I was back on the streetcar.

As I walked from my stop down the block toward the club, worldly men in tuxedos were standing outside the door, smoking and telling stories. I made my way downstairs, and stood in the back while my eyes got accustomed to the dark. There was no announcement, no official beginning of the show. The drummer and bass player wandered on stage and began adjusting their instruments, talking and laughing. The drummer picked up a pair of brushes, and they started vamping on a twelve-bar blues, just drums and bass. Presently, the tux-clad men from outside drifted in, in twos and threes, picked up their saxophones and trumpets, and fiddled idly with the reeds and mouthpieces. One of them stood up and started playing the blues on a tenor sax. After ten minutes, he was still playing, only now he was standing right in front of me, having traversed the whole club, snaking through the tables. He ignored the stage until, reaching the back wall, he turned back toward his fellows, and ratcheted up the intensity even higher. They responded by picking up their horns and blowing waves of swinging riffs, in four-part harmony, complete with great cascades of dissonant thirteenths.

I realized that, ten minutes into a show that hadn't ever actually started, the room was lifting off the ground. With no fanfare, Ellington himself appeared at the piano, shouting the tenor man's name: "Ladies and Gentlemen, Paul Gonsalves!" This chaotic scene continued while the band members sorted themselves out, finally coming to a thunderous final chord, thick with flat fives and sevens. Ellington leaned into the microphone, the picture of savoir-faire (a quality unknown in my world of unkempt hippiness) and said simply, "Ladies and gentlemen, we want you to know that we love you madly." He velvet-hammered the opening riff of "Take the A Train," and they were off again.

After an hour of invigorating chaos, I headed back to the dressing room to get one of the only two autographs I've ever asked for. Ellington signed my table tent on a makeshift desk that was actually a wardrobe trunk festooned with steamship stickers from around the world. Jazz was a living, breathing juggernaut of funk and swing. It was wild, just like rock. I wanted to go deeper and hear the stories that the tuxedo guys were sharing in their soulful melodies.

As final exams approached in May, my roommate Keith's gym/headphone regimen finally caught up with him. He realized that he was actually expected to take tests on the subjects listed on his registration form. Having skipped virtually all of his classes for the entire year, this raised a red flag. He turned to Joe, the smart one, for advice.

"Well, Keith, you should just go to the library, and stay there around the clock studying."

Keith looked relieved. "That's a great idea. Where is the library?" The library, which resembled Chartres Cathedral, was the largest building on campus.

"Those big buildings just down the hill from us? Okay, that's the campus. The really big one? Made of granite? That's the library."

Keith failed to ace the exams. Never one to wallow in pent-up feelings, he decided to gather up everything in the kitchen made of glass, pile it in the hallway, then spend the rest of the evening hurling stuff against the cinder block walls, while bellowing like an angry moose in rutting season. The whole floor stayed awake in observance. We couldn't have slept anyway, what with the bellowing and the real possibility of a Welch Hall mass murder putting an end to our college careers so close to summer vacation.

Keith was calm the next day, a moose the day *after* rutting season. I tried a little conversation.

"Keith, you're from New Jersey, right?"

"Yeah, Rutherford."

"I used to spend part of the summer in Jersey. There and New York City."

He snorted. "New York, eh?"

"Yeah, I loved New York growing up. Did you go there a lot as a kid, being right across the river?"

"Never been there in my life."

"You could see New York, but you never went over there?"

"You go over there, freakin' Ricans will kill you."

I fell silent. I knew what he meant, I suppose, having been almost killed by Keith's own flying beer mugs the night before. I rolled over in my bunk, realizing I'd gotten away from the KKK and the bigotry down south, only to meet up with it again in my own dorm room in erudite Boston. I was feeling a little homesick.

The semester was nearly over. I moved my mattress and a few basics down the hall to another basement dweller's room. All of us down in our catacomb circulated freely among the converted utility rooms. With no resident assistant, we were a law unto ourselves, so I was able to pack up and get out of range of any stray flying glassware.

My host was a fellow music lover who had the agreeable practice of staying up all night playing records on his turntable, eschewing sleep. That was fine with me, so I plopped my one-inch thick mattress down on the floor.

A couple of other guys gathered around as the records played. It was a night of passage. In a few days, our subterranean brotherhood would split up as we traveled back to our respective hometowns. For various reasons, some of us wouldn't return to Boston College. We were mostly silent, pensive. Bob Dylan's newly released album "New Morning" plopped down on the record changer, and his words, as usual, seemed to sum up our feelings at the moment. The next record was quietly announced as "the real stuff." A scratchy, wizened voice came creeping out of the little speaker, accompanied by a guitar that loped, then lurched, playing chords that were neither major nor minor. The words were strange and gothic. The singer was haunted by a hellhound, he wanted possession over judgment day, he foresaw some kind of hard rain coming, and he made his guitar sound like the wind blowing. I picked up the album sleeve and read the title: "Robert Johnson, King of the Delta Blues Singers." At 3:00 a.m., on the eve of a journey into the next phase of a youngster's life, it was scary stuff; scary but great. His voice drew me to the road like an otherworldly pied piper.

The night before school let out, my buddies Geno and Craig entreated me to take part in one last rock jam. Since we didn't know anyone else on campus who had a decent guitar, the jams consisted of me alone, plugging into my Marshall amp and playing every song I could muster. Geno and Craig would gesticulate wildly, striking iconic rock poses that rivaled Jimi Hendrix on his best nights. Hendrix had died during the school year, so I played all the songs from "Are You Experienced"—the songs that the Flying Hospital had labored to learn—and we toasted the great man of rock with quaffs of execrable Boone's Farm apple wine.

When I reached the end of my Hendrix repertoire, we boarded the streetcar for one last trip down to Kenmore Square for grinders at Boston House of Pizza. After that it was back up to Newton and a hike to the neighborhood bakery, where we knew the night-shift baker was willing to toss a few fresh donuts out to penniless college students. Then it was back to campus, marveling at the stars and planets, and cogitating on the fact that the heavenly bodies were "across" rather than "up." With that deep realization, we retired to our separate quarters for a few hours' sleep on the last night in Boston.

At dawn on the last day of the school year, I packed my few possessions into the Volkswagen, set aside the Grateful Dead's "American Beauty" for 8-track road music, and went back up the hill to work my final shift as Condiment Man in the dining hall. After the shift, I tossed my ketchup- and mustard-stained apron in the laundry chute, and that was it for Boston College. I fired up the four cylinders, pushed in the tape, and pointed the car west on the Mass Pike, toward America.

Chapter 4: Hitting the Road

I didn't go back to Boston College. My grades were okay, but I was focused on music. My clearest memories of the two semesters were Duke Ellington at the Jazz Workshop and Clarence White at the Boston Tea Party.

I knew that if I just quit school, it would mean failure for my mom and dad, so I struck a deal with them. If they let me drop out of Boston College, they could reabsorb the funds they had put aside for my higher education, and I would enroll part-time at George Mason University, a brash little up-and-coming school in Northern Virginia. I would pay my own way right up to graduation, as long as I could take my time getting there. It took ten years, but I held up my end of the deal, and I was genuinely proud when they both saw me get my diploma.

Hoping to demonstrate to my folks a formidable capacity for gainful employment, I auditioned for a few Top 40 bands. I found out that I was terrible at Top 40, which was fortunate because the gig, which required playing the exact parts from bland current records, singing in an ersatz Vegas belting style, and having carefully coiffed hair, was repellant to me. After a short stint on the notorious 14th Street nightclub strip, I bade farewell to that world, hoping something good would happen. It did.

Out in Falls Church, Virginia, a little shop opened up called Guitars Unlimited. I hung around and became friendly with the owner, a fellow named Don, who had recently moved from California. He told me that he used to give Jerry Garcia, who taught at Don's former shop in San Francisco, a few bucks for a hamburger when he was a starving musician. Don didn't have any expensive instruments for sale in Falls Church, so he didn't have the budget to hire a legitimate guitar repair person. I got the job, and I was foolishly confident enough to expand my repair practice to another shop, Giant Music, in South Arlington. I soon realized that I needed a mentor, because I actually knew very little about repairing guitars!

One day in July 1971, a customer brought in a Gretsch solid body electric. He wanted the frets replaced—all of them. I put the guitar in a corner and hoped he might forget about it and never come back. Unfortunately, he called a few weeks later, saying he was leaving town and needed to pick up the refretted guitar in forty-eight hours. I panicked, of course. Refretting is a master-level job. In desperation I called Don Downing.

Don was the mentor to any and all young rock musicians who were lucky enough to meet up with him. He lived in an apartment that was lined floor-to-ceiling with Fender amps and Fender and Gibson guitar cases. He traded instruments for a living, and he played six nights a week in the tough clubs down on the 14th Street strip. His stage name was Little Willie, and his band was The Hand Jives. I had spent hours at his place, soaking up wisdom about rock and roll, and marveling at the fact that there actually *was* wisdom about rock and roll. My last chance to get the Gretsch sorted out was a call to Willie. He was, as always, cool, calm, and collected. "No problem, man. I've got a boy over in Prince George's County who does guitar repairs like you wouldn't believe. If you ever have a guitar you want to sell, leave it with him overnight, and when you get it back, you won't want to sell it anymore." He gave me Danny Gatton's number.

Danny actually answered the phone in those days, a practice he abandoned later on. "Sure. Just bring it on over now." I beat it around the Beltway and found his apartment. He put the guitar on the dining room table, which doubled as his workbench. "Come back in a couple of hours." It was 2:00 p.m., so I went somewhere and came back at 4:00. The guitar was not only done, it was better than new. My job was saved, and I started bringing him any repairs that I couldn't pull off myself. For the rest of that year, he never said a word about playing the guitar, and while I figured he probably knew some chords, it seemed that he was mainly a handyman who could fix anything. Besides guitars, there were always parts of cars, air conditioners, etc., lying around. He certainly didn't look the part of a rock star.

In January 1972, I had a guitar repair job for Danny, and he said on the phone, "I'm playing a gig out in Virginia tonight. Why don't you just bring it there?" I was surprised to hear that he played gigs on guitar. The place was in a strip mall in Herndon, which was still a small village in a mostly rural area. The club was actually two adjacent storefronts with blacked-out shop windows. You entered through The Web, and then went through another door to The Pussycat Lounge if you wanted to hear the band. They were on a break when I handed off the guitar. I was getting ready to leave, but I decided to stay for one song, just for laughs. These country guys were not rockers, for sure.

Danny strapped on a 1952 Telecaster, which to me was just an old guitar, and he plugged into a tweed Fender amp, which looked to me like a small suitcase. I had seen Hendrix, Clapton, and Beck, all in 1968, and they didn't use little suitcase amps. My snobbishness turned to shock when Danny hit the first lick, the intro to "Mystery Train." That moment is still prophetic to me, because that lick is one of the keys to Danny's style, as well as the tune that some say is the foundation of rock and roll. The whole world of Telecaster tone and technique was encompassed in that little passage. It hit me all at once. I was literally numb. After all the rock concerts I'd been to, here I was in a little bar in Virginia, and the guitarist was completely blowing away anything I'd ever heard. Almost everything he played was unfamiliar, yet it was all great. I couldn't figure out any of it from where I sat. I knew instantly that this sound and approach was going to be a big part of my life; it was clear that, while I was never going to play music on this guy's level, the attempt would pull me in the right direction.

Because we had been friends for half a year before I knew Danny played, there was always an element of trust between us. That became more important later on, when he was surrounded by people who wanted something from him, some of them good people and some not so good. He wasn't a great judge of that, so he was comfortable around his older friends. That gave me a chance to be of service to him on occasion over the next two decades, although helping him out was not always an easy matter. For the next several years, I went out two or three nights a week to hear Danny in small bars around the Beltway. I was usually the only person listening to the band, although I began to meet a few other young people like myself who had stumbled across this genius, right here in our home town. The craziest part was that we already had a guitar genius, Roy Buchanan, in the same neighborhood! So it was sheer luck to love the guitar and also be born and raised in D.C. at that time.

A few years later, Danny took a job with Liz Meyer and Friends, a great country rock band in D.C. Liz played at the Childe Harold, where hip music fans hung out, and Danny's reputation took off. As a matter of fact, Bruce Springsteen, who wielded a Les Paul with hard rock intensity when we gigged with him back in 1970, shared a bill at the Childe Harold with Danny. Suddenly Bruce was playing an old Telecaster through an Echoplex into a tweed Fender Bassman—the exact Gatton setup. Danny's influence was beginning to spread.

The early 1970s were a time of wide-open exploration for a kid raised on the British Invasion and a subscription to *The Village Voice*. I knew that there was a whole world of real folk and roots music out there, like a vast, mysterious Narnia, just waiting for me to find the right portal to reveal its secrets. The movie *Deliverance* was a glimpse. So was the album, "Will the Circle be Unbroken," and the Sun rockabilly stuff that Gatton was playing was another entrée into that world. I bought records, but I wanted to get all the way in: to hear, and see, the real folks playing this stuff—bluegrass, blues, rockabilly, mountain music.

Growing up in the D.C. area, I was aware that the region had, since the 1940s, drawn migrants from all over the South as the federal government grew into an ever-expanding bureaucracy that offered workers stability and benefits. The migrants brought their homegrown music with them, and the city and its surrounding suburbs were a panoply of roots music blending the country and bluegrass traditions with blues, gospel, and jazz. I was drawn to all of it, and I wanted to be around the artists who had the real essence. Festivals were an opportunity to do that, which meant that mobility was essential to a young gypsy hitting the festival circuit. So, I traded my first car, a classic Volkswagon "Bug," for an even more classic Volkswagon Microbus. Now I could hit the road on a moment's notice with all the essentials of life on board. When I was offered a job volunteering at the Ohio Folk Festival, I grabbed my acoustic guitar, threw a few things in my backpack, and sped off (40 mph was speeding in a Microbus). I was back on the road, this time with a car instead of my thumb.

The mountains, and by that I mean the Alleghenies, not even the Rockies, were always problematic for the horsepower-challenged '63 VW bus. Long upgrades were not only slow going, they were downright embarrassing, as Amish buggies whizzed by me disdainfully. After struggling up the eastern slope of the Appalachians in first gear, it occurred to me that reverse probably had more torque than first. For the rest of my traveling days with the VW, I would "do a 180" on long upgrades and climb the slopes backwards. I installed a new-fangled 8-track player in the old van, and when I accelerated, the music sped up. When I braked, the music slowed down. That seemed to make perfect sense, and only endeared me even more to my clunky iron horse.

In Athens, Ohio, where the festival was being staged in the basketball arena, I jumped at the chance to man the instrument check booth. This was central to the backstage, and every performer would, at some point, drop off their guitars for safekeeping while they schmoozed and relaxed between shows. Of course, I stashed my own flattop in the back, just in case jamming broke out.

It was a great weekend. Earl Scruggs had just put together a new band with his sons, carrying Dobro legend Uncle Josh Graves over from the classic Flatt and Scruggs lineup. John Hartford had Norman Blake on lead guitar, and Tom Rush had Trevor Veitch playing a vintage Telecaster. Arlo Guthrie, riding high on the pop charts at the time, brought what seemed like an army of Nashville pickers with him. They sat behind him, like Duke Ellington's band, rising on Arlo's cue to take hot bluegrass solos that dumbfounded us rock and rollers. Jim Seals and Dash Crofts amazed the crowd by perfectly reproducing their complex pop hits. They came out for their encore armed with a tenor sax, at which point Seals proceeded to tear the roof off with a Coltrane-style free improvisation.

Some of the best moments were the solo acts. Songwriter Eric Andersen made the arena feel like an intimate coffeehouse. Townes Van Zandt kept the same vibe rolling. Eric sang a couple of songs by Merle Haggard and they hit hard. When he sang, "I turned twenty-one in prison, doin' life without parole" I wondered if any of the other collegiate young people in the audience had spent time in a Kansas jail. The next act, John Hammond Jr., gave the crowd a clinic on how a single guitar, in the hands of a right and righteous player, can rock any size crowd as hard as a whole band. He played a bunch of songs by the shadowy legend, Robert Johnson; the ghostly songs that I'd heard in a basement in Boston a year or so earlier. Now they were live, and Hammond sang and played with a drive and fury that was stunning. "If I had possession over judgement day," "I've got a hellhound on my trail," and the apocalyptic "You better come in my kitchen, 'cause it's gonna be rainin' outdoors." The songs chilled me to the bone. It was a weekend to soak up music like a sponge, and I was happily exhausted by midnight on Saturday night. I dug my guitar out of the stack of guitar cases, and headed over to the dorm that served as the performer and crew quarters.

Walking down the dark hall of the dorm, around midnight, I heard a fiddle playing in one of the rooms. The door was slightly ajar, and I peered in. Vassar Clements was sitting on his bed alone, eyes closed, with his ever-present pipe clenched between his teeth. Pouring out of his fiddle was music of a kind that I had never heard before. At such close range, its power was overwhelming and joyful. Like any brash kid, I ran to my room and grabbed my guitar. When I sat down and started "beating rhythm," Vassar's tanned-leather face crinkled in a slight smile, but his eyes stayed closed. He didn't need to see anything. He could probably tell from my groove that I was more of a rocker than a bluegrass cat, so he segued into "Norwegian Wood." It wasn't like Lennon's lilting waltz, though. It was driving, ancient; the way Coltrane and Hendrix might have jammed on it. Following Vassar through the landscape of his improvisation was like following a Sherpa up the Himalayas. Everything was new to me, and my own instrument seemed to open up to wider and wider vistas. Before long, Randy Scruggs and Jody Maphis had poked their heads in, and they ran for their guitars. Pretty soon the little room was packed and rocking. "Norwegian Wood" segued into something else, and something else again, and Vassar never opened his eyes. He just spun out a tale like the Odyssey, told by a fiddle; like a Bach fugue, but totally spontaneous, happening in a luminous moment that lasted all night.

As the session finally wound down, we all stumbled, laughing, out into the sunrise. Sleep was pointless. Across the street, Eric Andersen and Townes Van Zandt were sipping coffee at a sidewalk café, basking in their own aura of cool, ignoring the hot summer sun beating down on their black suits. As for me, I'd gotten a ticket to Narnia, and my life was changed once again by the transcendent energy of music.

I liked life in Athens, Ohio. It was a small town in a rural area, but it was populated with smart university people. I'd gotten the call to work the festival from one of my best buddies, Vander Lockett. Like me, he grew up in Arlington. We played in bands together, including some rough clubs in D.C. where the band members grew tight as a protective fraternity. Life in Athens wasn't tough. It was easy, and cool things happened. One night I drove out into the country to a tiny movie theater, which was having live music that night. The music was Chuck Berry, and he tore the roof off.

I decided to hang around Athens, and Vander scored us another gig, playing in a free jazz ensemble called The Intergalactic Space Spies. Michael Guilford, who also headed up the Jazz Studies department at Ohio University, fronted the group. I slept on the floor of Mike's living room, surrounded by his record collection, and I was free to play jazz records all day. I learned a lot about music and about being a musician from Mike and the other guys in the band. We played concerts on campus, art openings, and poetry readings where we improvised behind the authors. We listened as a band to records, especially Miles Davis and John Coltrane. As time went on, I felt that free improv was a way of opening all the musical channels, after which I was at liberty to play any style, including simpler, more organic sounds. I wanted to get back to exploring the structure and vibe of roots music, the stuff I had heard at The Pussycat Lounge. Vander left town to go on tour, hanging out with Leo Kottke, who was playing small college coffeehouses. I was getting rambling fever again.

One night I packed my guitar and amp in the VW bus and took off from Athens, heading east over icy roads to Boston. I looked up Jim Farrell, an old friend from folk mass. He was an excellent singer and a larger-than-life personality. He'd been touring with the Broadway show *Hair* for years, and I knew he would be in Boston where the show was running. I looked him up at the Eliot Hotel off of Kenmore Square, and the floor of his suite became my next bunk on the road.

One afternoon, Jim and I were down in the theater district, walking past the Boston Music Hall, when someone called him from an alleyway. It was a roadie who had worked for *Hair* on tour. He beckoned to us to come down the alley to the Music Hall stage door. "There's somebody I want you to meet." As we went into the theater, I heard the opening piano notes of the song, "Blue." Joni Mitchell was sitting at the piano. The roadie introduced Jim and me. I was in a bit of shock, having been absent-mindedly walking down the street not two minutes earlier, so I stammered something and backed away awkwardly. She seemed very nice, but what do you say to Joni Mitchell, especially after you just interrupted her warm-up: "How about those Red Sox?" Her manager, Elliot Roberts, gave us tickets to the show that night, which featured an unknown opening act named Jackson Browne.

After *Hair* closed in Boston, Jim went north and I went down to Virginia to see if my family still remembered who I was. Vander had wound up his Leo Kottke duties, so of course we decided to get a band going. The band, Grendel, already existed, but Vander and I moved in and took up residence. We were a tight group. We worked a lot, hindered only by the fact that our organist had a Hammond B3 and two Leslie tone cabinets, a massive schlep at each gig. Vander and I began to lobby for a steady gig. We found one at a place called The Godfather, over in D.C. The name tells you all you need to know about the place. The other band members nearly mutinied when they found out we had to wear matching suits, but professionalism and empty bank books prevailed, and we took the gig. We got even tighter from playing every night, but eventually, with all of us being young and single, with little responsibility, we realized that none of us wanted a steady job, and the band broke up.

The highway beckoned, and I wound up once again on Jim Farrell's floor, although he was now in New York City, up near the Natural History Museum. We lived next door to Jesus, or at least Billy Grey, who was playing the lead in *Jesus Christ, Superstar.* The tenants on our floor were all Broadway people, and we got along like a little social club, sharing meals and going out to the beach on Long Island. The trade-off for my lodging was that I played guitar whenever Jim got a folk singing gig. We did various things around the Village at the Metro, Kenny's Castaways, The Bitter End, and so on, but the only steady work we could find was at a little corner place on Bleecker Street called The Back Fence. The pay was ten dollars a night, split between the two of us. That wasn't exactly a living wage in Manhattan, so we started auditioning for road gigs. Our first audition in New York was for The College Coffeehouse Circuit. We got the job. They sent us all over the country playing, you guessed it, college coffeehouses.

One night, we were booked into the student lounge at the University of Pittsburgh. We were put up in a large hotel near the campus. We waited in line to check in behind the members of a rock band who were decked out head to toe in leopard skin, fur coats, and feather boas. It was Mott the Hoople. They were playing the same night at the Syrian Mosque, a cavernous venue nearby. After Jim and I played our coffeehouse gig, we hiked over to the loading dock of the Mosque, which put us right behind the stage. Leaning back against the dumpsters, we could hear the show pretty well. Afterwards, we were in our hotel room, playing guitars and singing some Everly Brothers songs, when there came a knock on the door. I expected it to be a hotel employee telling us to quit singing at midnight. Instead, it was two young ladies, arrayed in sartorial splendor that was similar to the band with whom we had shared a check-in moment earlier in the day. The looks on their faces could only be described as crestfallen. They glanced sideways at one another, and then one of them, the spokeswoman, addressed us, as one might address a piece of cheese that is found to be moldy. "Oh. You're not Mott the Hoople." There was no good response except. "Sorry!" They continued the search for their preferred after-party. Folk music, sans leopard skin and feather boas, has never been a groupie magnet.

We made lots of friends on the college circuit, did some hard touring by Greyhound bus, and made a little bit of money doing original songs. The "little bit" of money eventually became problematic, and we made our way down to D.C. where we could stay in my parents' basement for a while.

In D.C., we heard that there was a new passenger train that went to Florida every day, and it was going to have music on board. We auditioned and got the job. It was steady work, although a little bit different from any other gig I've had. We played on the upper level of one of the old Santa Fe Super Chief observation cars. It was a beautiful piece of gear, except that the Auto Train brand required that everything, including the railroad cars, had to be painted purple. The stage was tiny. As a matter of fact, the neck of my guitar extended over the top of the stairway leading down to the bar. After a few drinks, the patrons would simply grab the neck of my guitar like a subway turnstile and lift it up so they could navigate their way downstairs. Did I clarify that they did this *while* I was playing? It was a good exercise in staying focused.

As the train made its way south, and the patrons made their way to the bar, they began to shout for a current hit song, "For the Good Times." It's a fine song, written by Kris Kristofferson, but we didn't know it. It occurred to us, that aside from the occasional shout in our direction, no one was listening very closely. We decided we'd sing any old song, maybe even one that Jim wrote, and end it by singing, in an earnest voice, "for the good times." That was met with thunderous applause, since they seemed to think we must have sung the entire song.

Being steadily employed on the train, and hoping to relieve my parents from lodging a couple of musicians, Jim and I went our separate ways, although we both ended up on different farms in Rappahannock County, Virginia. The train employees popu-lated the farms around Front Royal and Sperryville; we worked two or three days a week, and had time off in between runs. I lived with two of the train porters on an eight-hundred acre farm with horses, cows, a pond, and a reclusive combat vet who lived in a tent over the hill with a dog name "Fubar." Larry, Mark, and I split the one hundred-fifty dollar monthly rent. We bunked in a pre-Civil War era log cabin. When you looked through the chinks in the grout between the logs, you were looking outside. No insulation, just a fireplace in every room. I got tired of the farm and tired of the train, so when my '63 Corvair died on a winding country road, I gave it away and hitched a ride back to D.C. in the tow truck.

Chapter 5: Rockin' the Symphony

I bought a massive Chevy Townsman station wagon, the kind with the backward facing rear bench seat, and I started gathering instruments together to do freelance backup work. With that goal in mind, I took my little Harmony "batwing" mandolin out to the Red Fox Tavern in Bethesda, Maryland. The Red Fox featured Emmylou Harris and the Angel Band one night a week, The Seldom Scene on another night, a national act on weekends, and an acoustic jam on Monday nights. The acoustic jam featured the top folk musicians in town. Fortunately, I didn't know that, so I played with complete confidence, and sang a song I had heard Ry Cooder do, "How Can I Poor Man Stand Such Times and Live?" The place went nuts. I'd *never* made a place go nuts. It made a great impact on my self-confidence to discover that I could get up on a stage alone and entertain a crowd for a few minutes. I joined a jug band, played lots of concerts, ate Chinese food with my newfound friends, and generally loved the world of folk music. Of course, nothing paid, so the old predicament came around again. I was enjoying my gigs and I had time off to do things like see jazz pianist Bill Evans play an inspiring small gig in Maryland, but nights off don't pay a musician's bills. I needed to find work and as luck would have it, it found me.

I played the Red Fox on Mondays without fail, working up different songs every week. Toward the end of the year, I was casting around for a secular holiday song to play as a chord/melody solo on guitar. I settled on "Silver Bells," and I wondered how the jazzy changes would go over with the folk crowd. They liked it fine, and I was packing up my axe when a pipe-smoking stranger approached me. "I'm Chip Cliff. You play really well. You should be working." In my mid-twenties, I had just quit a two-year gig playing on a passenger train, and I was considering retiring as a down-and-out gentleman farmer in the foothills of the Blue Ridge. Chip cut right to the chase: "The first thing you need is a teaching gig. Do you teach banjo?" I played banjo, but I had never taught banjo, or anything else. Before I could formulate a response, Chip settled the matter.

"Be at Ellsworth Studios at 10 a.m. on Monday. They need a banjo teacher. I'll tell them you're coming."

"But what'll I teach?"

Chip tamped the tobacco in his bowl. "Just show up. All you have to do is know more than the students!"

On this slim thread, I began my teaching career. The Ellsworths, a family of concert violinists, fortunately had no idea what constituted a qualified banjo teacher, so I got the job. For the first few weeks, I simply arrived early, read the next few pages in the Pete Seeger banjo book, and taught those pages. That kept me a week ahead of my students until, after a year or so, I'd been through all the current banjo, guitar, and mandolin methods, and was starting to arrive at enough ideas of my own to become a real teacher. I stayed there for six years, teaching about twenty students a week.

Now that I was a bona fide teacher at a real music school, Chip brought me along further into the world of professional music. He had decided that he would mentor me, and made me his protégé. Since almost everything he knew was something that I didn't know, it was a perfect match. He was amazingly generous with his time and his knowledge, and he had a brash sense of total self-confidence that was the cornerstone of what he did for a living, playing freelance guitar. He not only taught me a myriad of skills, but he also inculcated that confidence in me.

A freelance guitarist basically hangs out a shingle saying, "I will play whatever you need on guitar, in any situation that you throw at me." It sounds like high pressure, and it is, but it's also a constant process of intense learning.

Chip taught me all kinds of things I never would have discovered on my own. Sight-reading was one of those things. That's reading a chart up to tempo the first time, without practicing it or even seeing it previously. It involves different skills: reading melodies, chords, odd time signatures, counting measures when you're not playing so you'll come back in at the right spot, and following a conductor's baton instead of a drummer. These are all things that would never come up in a rock band or backing a singer-songwriter, and they opened up a broader world of music to me. I can honestly say that meeting Chip at the Red Fox was a moment that changed my life. I knew from then on that I could always make a living with my guitar. I would never have to quit, and that was all-important to me.

In order to do freelance work at venues with union stagehands, I had to belong to the Musician's Union. This would also give me health insurance and a pension plan, so I went down to the union hall, a small house on Wisconsin Avenue in D.C. There, I met with Sam Jack Kaufman, the president of the local. He was an entertainer from the vaudeville era, and before we got down to business, he pulled out his scrapbook and regaled me with stories about the great old days. Finally, it was time to audition.

I got my guitar, and figuring that standard songs were the meat and potatoes of the union, I started playing "The Girl from Ipanema." Sam Jack waved for me to stop. "That's great," he said, "But can you play any rock music?" I quickly tried to imagine a vaudeville musician's idea of rock music, and I played the intro to "Proud Mary." Sam Jack nearly jumped out of his chair. "That's great! You're exactly what we need!" I signed on various dotted lines, and then it was time for my initiation. I was instructed to go into the basement and take a seat on the couch. There, a slide show would play, describing the benefits of union membership. I went down and took a seat on the couch, next to the only other initiate that day. It was Emmylou Harris. We watched the slide-show. Afterwards, the union people seemed to have all gone to lunch, so we made our way out the front door. On the stoop, she told me she was heading down to Austin to play Armadillo World Headquarters, a legendary music venue. Then she would continue on to Los Angeles, where, as she put it, she had her fingers crossed, because it looked like she might have a record deal. That certainly worked out well, and it was a source of pride for the Red Fox family of musicians that she became the once and future Queen of Country Music.

Now that I had a union card, it was time to do some work, and I started getting calls right away. They were usually prefaced with, "Chip Cliff gave me your number and he says you can play___." Whatever they said I could play, I simply agreed and then figured out how to play it. My motto became, "It's great to be the worst person in the group, because you are learning from everybody else, even as you annoy the heck out of them." I had never, for example, played in certain configurations before, including any kind of orchestra. That was all about to change.

The phone rang. "Pete? This is Dave Bragunier."

"Hi, Dave." I didn't actually know him.

"Pete, I'm the contractor for the National Symphony Orchestra. We've got a major concert coming up at the Kennedy Center. Aaron Copland will conduct his Third Symphony, and his protégé, David Del Tredici, is going to conduct the world premiere of his new piece, the 'Lobster Quadrille' from his 'Final Alice.' I'm looking for a player who is expert on the mandolin, can follow a conductor, and can sight-read an orchestra part."

Since I was woefully deficient at the entire skill set he had just outlined, I answered without hesitation; "I'm your man."

"Excellent!" He gave me the rehearsal dates and times. I hung up and surveyed the situation. This was either a great break or a potential public flogging. Either way, it was the essence of free-lancing. Accept a gig you're not really qualified for, then work your tail off to actually be qualified by the time the downbeat rolls around.

I got to the Kennedy Center early for the first rehearsal. There was a secure underground entrance and tunnel, a maze of dressing rooms, wardrobe rooms, prop workshops, rehearsal rooms, and a full-sized cafeteria peopled with ballerinas, operatic prima donnas in full costume, and tough stagehands. I found my way through the James Bond-style labyrinth to the concert hall and stepped out onto the stage. I tried to keep cool and look around for my chair, but I couldn't help but sneak a glance out at the house. Huge. So many seats. So many balconies. So much red velvet. And it would all come crashing down if my little mandolin wasn't up to snuff.

Snuff was pretty high on that stage. Everyone else undoubt-edly had graduated from Juilliard. Aaron Copland was unassum-ing, but he carried the gravitas of his lifetime of triumphs and Yale lectures as an unmistakable aura. Del Tredici, on the other hand, was a dashing John F. Kennedy lookalike who wore a black turtleneck and cracked jokes easily with the orchestra members. No one was threatening, and Dave Bragunier welcomed me warmly. Chip was unpacking a tenor banjo. He introduced me to Carmen, the top accordionist in town. The three of us were to constitute a mock Italian café band, playing in the midst of the larger orchestra. I sat down and looked at the music. The nota-tion at the top read "Mandolin ignores key and time signature of the rest of the orchestra." Perfect! That's probably what I would have done, anyway.

I sat out for the Copland portion and watched the elderly, able man at work. Then it was my turn. As the chairs were rear-ranged, the principal violinist passed me in the wings and bowed deeply; "I solisti." Yup, that's me. He had a twinkle in his eye and his tongue in cheek, but I also knew that I would have my flatpick handed to me in a few minutes if I didn't keep my wits about me. For a brief moment, I wished I had done a couple of seasons on the farm team instead of jumping right from playing "Johnny B. Goode" at local bars to The National Symphony. I took a deep breath and tuned my instrument.

Del Tredici walked to the podium, raised his baton, smiled, and hit the downbeat. The music was chaotic in a cool way, very modern, not entirely unmelodic, although I found the melodies to be like sand traps when you're reading the chart. You can't be seduced by anything anyone else plays in the orchestra, or you'll lose your own place, and you're back on the Auto Train, not to mention wasting a lot of expensive union orchestra time.

Fortunately, when we got to our section of the piece, chaos was the desired effect. The mandolin was required to play long, tremulous notes of somewhat indeterminate length. Hallelujah! No matter what I did, I couldn't throw anybody off! Even if I did play something "wrong," they were all ignoring us, anyway, counting measures until their next entrance.

The actual concert went off without a hitch, and I was initiated into the world of symphony freelancing. Dave Bragunier stopped me in the hall and said "Thanks, I'll be calling you." I was now a sometime symphony cat.

Now that I was working with real classical players, I turned my attention for the first time to classical guitar. I bought a "student model" Ramirez, made in Spain, and called on Sophocles Pappas. He was retired, but was still one of the dominant figures in classical guitar at the time. He was the original owner of The Guitar Shop in downtown D.C., back when guitar meant classical and jazz. That's where, in the early 1960s, Segovia, Julian Bream, John Williams, Barney Kessel, or Wes Montgomery might be found, hanging out and talking guitar. I had taken a few lessons there from jazz hotshot Frank Mullin, who practiced on a Ramirez using a thick felt pick, so that when he switched to electric he could play at warp speed. As for Pappas, he no longer went into D.C., but he was available to meet with young guitarists at his house out in Fairfax. He was an old school mentor in the European tradition, which meant that you summoned up your courage to see him, and then he decided if you'd gain access to the classical guitar community or not. It was harsh, but that was the way that it was done.

I sat down and Pappas handed me a concert, not student, model Ramirez. They are set up to project loudly in a big hall, which means very high string action, difficult to play. I played a little bit of Bach's "Bourrée in E minor," which is the "Louie, Louie" of classical guitar: so easy anyone can struggle through it. Pappas endured that, and said, "Play something else. Not Bach!" I played the first few bars of "Recuerdos de l'Alhambra," a virtuoso piece well beyond my ability. He stopped me. "Fine. I will put you with a teacher." He scribbled a phone number and ushered me out the door. I gathered that I must have passed the audition.

The number was for Larry Snitzler, who taught in an apartment above Dupont Circle in D.C. Larry had just returned from a number of years as a protégé of Segovia's over in Europe, under the patronage of a certain Count Chigi. He and his wife were charming people, and I enjoyed their patois that combined English, French, Spanish, and Italian, but I chafed under the slow process of learning classical guitar. I would play a single note for the entire lesson, with Larry good-naturedly shaking his head, and once in a while nodding, "That was a good one." At this time, I was working six nights a week in a show band down on the waterfront, a job that required fast reading and listening skills, and the repeating of single notes, going for a perfection of tone, was too slow for the way my mind worked at the time.

I decided to see if a full-time college degree in guitar might progress at a faster rate, so my next audition was with John Marlowe, the head of the American University Classical Guitar degree program. I went to his office and played a little bit. He smiled and said, "Yes. I would accept you into the degree program." He handed me an extensive repertoire list. "But, there is one thing I require. For four years, you will do nothing but work on this list. No popular music, no jazz, no paying gigs of any kind." I thanked him and he let me keep the list. I still work from it today, but only when I feel like playing a little bit of classical. I hate to think of all that I would have missed if I had taken him up on the offer.

What I really wanted to do during this period was not only work, but also keep getting better on all styles of guitar. Snitzler was imposing some classical discipline, and Chip kept sending commercial gigs my way, giving me tips on how to get through them. I decided to supplement this tutelage with one-off lessons, whenever I could get them, with master players—true artists— when they came through town. My first attempt at this came up when Joe Pass, who was arguably the all-time greatest jazz guitarist, came to D.C. for a three-night gig in Georgetown.

Blues Alley, the venerable D.C. jazz club, had the atmosphere one night of a Tibetan monastery when the high lama pays a visit. The place was packed to the rafters with long-haired kids, mostly male, and all of them guitarists. Onstage, Joe Pass was blowing everybody's mind. We were all rock and rollers in the audience. We couldn't have played the rhythm chords to "Cherokee" if our lives depended on it. Here he was, spinning out chorus after chorus of beautiful improvisation on those twisting changes, each chorus a melody in itself, just as strong as the original composer's. No band, not even drums and bass; just a guitar plugged into a tiny amp.

After the set, guys gathered around, asking questions about strings and so forth. I waited until the end, and then got up my courage.

"Mr. Pass, would you be willing to give a lesson tomorrow morning?"

He lit a cigar. "Call me Joe. It's gonna cost you."

I took that for a yes. "Okay, how much?"

"Fifty bucks." That was a lot for a guitar lesson in those days, but this *was* Joe Pass.

"You're on."

"All right, then. Be at the Holiday Inn at 10:00 a.m."

I was there at ten sharp. I called up to Joe's room. I woke him up. After a few minutes he remembered, probably with some regret, his promise of the night before. "Okay, give me fifteen minutes, and then come on up."

I gave him twenty, and then knocked on the door. In his suit pants from the night before, and a sleeveless white tee shirt, he looked frail, like the old men you see hanging around the cigar-rolling stand on Arthur Avenue in the Bronx. But he was a survivor, and there was an unmistakable air of toughness about him. He took his guitar out of a well-worn leather gig bag, and we sat down to play.

"So," he began, "You play pretty good, right? Rock and stuff?" I nodded hesitantly, searching for a balance between wanting to impress but also showing humble respect. Joe puffed on his cigar, then he spoke.

"I tell you what. I'll play a chord, and you play some lead over it. Whatever you wanna play." He played an E#9, the "Hendrix" chord.

This was my shot. No matter how shy or humble a guitarist may be, they turn into a giant when someone plays an E#9 chord. I grabbed the 12th fret and worked it, spinning sinuous licks that snaked across the fretboard like coiling cobras, striking on the flat five, and then the flat third, bending a full minor third and applying a wailing vibrato. I played every lick I knew over that chord. Silence settled over the hotel room.

"Very nice," said Joe. "You play real nice." Then he changed the subject, and told stories for a while. They were sprinkled with advice, the kind of advice that comes from decades of experience, not from books.

After ten minutes or so of this, he absentmindedly looked up from his guitar. "Uh, y'know that chord I played a little while ago?"

"Sure, the E#9."

"Yeah, that's it. I'll tell you what. I'm gonna play it again, and this time, play the exact same thing you played the last time." He had me.

"Okay, you got me. I can't do it. I can play some stuff, but I don't remember exactly what I played before."

"That's 'cause you didn't play a melody. Your fingers played a bunch of licks, but you weren't singing! What you gotta do is sing a melody in your head, and then play that."

In one cunning move, this guy opened up the whole soloing thing. It was all so clear. It wasn't about licks or riffs. You just learn the scales that go with chords, and then you sing melodies! Ten minutes and, boom, lesson done. Fifty bucks well spent.

Joe talked some more, and he played some beautiful little solo improvs that sounded like Debussy or Ravel, except that he was making them up as he went along. Offstage, he was a much more impressionistic, Bill Evans-type player than the barn burner who had peeled the paint off the walls of Blues Alley the previous night.

I drove home in a state of heightened awareness. This was a real teacher; that is, a real player who has the skeleton keys on his chain. He doesn't have to teach you any techniques, or give you any homework. He just hands you one of the keys and says, "You know what to do with this. Now get outta here." I left a new player.

Another great guitarist and great musician with whom I was lucky enough to study was Johnny Smith. I had found his eponymous "black album" back in 1971. I didn't know who he was, but I loved the photo of a Gibson guitar inside the jacket. The music was straight-ahead standards, but the guitar tone and phrasing was so perfect and beautiful that I felt really moved by it, the way I did so long ago when I heard The Ventures play "Walk, Don't Run" (which, coincidentally, was composed by Johnny Smith). Somehow his playing seemed to be a crucial piece of the guitar puzzle. He did everything right musically and there was never a note that I didn't agree with. That's rare!

It was about 1974 when I saw a very small advertisement in *Guitar Player* magazine for "The Johnny Smith Seminar." I had been looking for an avenue to take me away from imitating "Cream Live at the Fillmore," since everyone else was already covering that ground, and Johnny's sound and phrasing was the signpost. I made my way to River Edge, New Jersey, a suburb of New York.

Johnny took over a music store in River Edge for five consecutive weekdays, and his clear explanations and constant demonstrations created a mental template for me that totally opened up the neck of the guitar. At the end of each session, he would play a mini-concert of solo tunes. He combined jazz standards with contemporary classical harmonies, and played with his trademark touch and taste. When he played Debussy's "The Girl with the Flaxen Hair," I resolved that if I could ever play that on the guitar, with its deceptively simple pentatonic theme that skips seamlessly through several keys, I would consider that my major life accomplishment. I still play it every day.

Chapter 6: *Your Costume's in the Back*

I realize with my descriptions of inspiring and edifying gigs and lessons, I'm neglecting the other end of the spectrum, and yes, there is another end of the spectrum. Musicians all trade tales of "gigs from hell." Some of mine begin with the words, "Your costume's in the back."

I got a call to play a gig at a farm in Maryland that was rented out for weddings and various corporate events. I had played gigs there before, but this call was a little unusual. There was a band already hired, but they needed me to sing one song, "Misty." If I could do it, they would pay the full three-hour scale. Of course I could do it! When I arrived, the event coordinator told me, "Your costume's in the back." I found the employee locker room, where they had carefully laid out a set of German lederhosen for me. After donning the outfit, I was instructed to wait for a signal, at which point I would walk on stage and stand on a hay bale that would be preset for me. At the appointed time, the house lights went down, I walked out and climbed onto the hay bale in my lederhosen and sang "Misty" to enthusiastic applause. Then I changed back into my street clothes and thanked the client for making such careful preparations. I left, never knowing who the audience was, or why, from a vast array of entertainment options, they wanted to hear a guy in lederhosen sing "Misty" on a bale of hay.

A few months later, I got a typical freelance phone call, asking if I was free at a certain time on a certain day. The only details were to bring a banjo and dress however I wanted. The gig was during the day at an address near Fredericksburg, Virginia. I had musician friends down there, so I called Jimmy Arnold to let him know I had a gig in town. Jimmy was a brilliant natural player who could pick up any stringed instrument and play it at the top of the craft. He had strong ideas about music and scorned anything that he thought was a commercial sellout. I was looking forward to hanging out with him. When I arrived at the address, it turned out to be a fast food place. I went inside and found the manager, who told me, "Your costume's in the back." I was expecting a set of lederhosen, but instead, they had provided me with a huge dragon costume, the kind that mascots wear at a football game. The gloves were massive claws, and the entire outfit seemed to weigh about sixty pounds.

I was only able to shuffle about very slowly, struggling to stay upright and trying not to knock anyone down with my tail. My banjo technique gave new meaning to the style "claw hammer." As I shuffled, I saw Jimmy Arnold come in the front door. He looked around, expecting to see me somewhere. I made my way over to him as fast as I could stagger and I shouted, "Jimmy, it's me, Pete. I'm inside the dragon!" I shouted as loud as I could, but I realized that my voice was totally swallowed up by the thick layers of scales. It probably sounded like a mosquito buzzing to Jimmy. I was also flailing with my claws on the banjo, obscuring my tiny attempts to draw his attention. Seeing only fast food and an annoying dragon mascot bearing down on him, Jimmy turned heel and got out of there. I never saw him again, but I'm safe in the knowledge that, since we had just finished some finely-wrought studio work a few weeks prior, he never imagined that the tiny voice calling his name was me, inside the dragon.

There is an unspoken rule among freelancers that you just do the gig, with no complaints or inappropriate commentary. The music, good or bad, is important enough to someone that they hired professional musicians, so you treat the client with respect, and when they point you to the dragon costume you put it on and play. Very different from a rock band, where arguing and jockeying for power can be the normal order of the day. I liked doing these freelance type of gigs because they were oftentimes true variety shows, with comedians, jugglers, opera singers, and sometimes a magician who would saw a woman in half while we vamped on a diminished chord. It was a refuge for old vaudeville acts that were still working a circuit. At one particular show, I was backing Jerry Murad's Harmonicats playing their 1950s hit, "Peg O' My Heart" and some other selections on a variety of harmonicas, one of which seemed to be almost the size of a Volkswagen. I had been gigging so much that I was exhausted, and in my tired state, I actually fell asleep during one of their songs and woke up about sixteen bars later in the tune. I must have played okay, because none of the Harmonicats looked askance at me.

The calls kept coming thick and fast. On a typical day, I would get to Bias Studios at 9:00 a.m. for a jingle session. That would involve sitting down, tuning up, reading a thirty second chart a couple of times, and then packing up so the horn players could start at 9:30. I was third call for studio work behind John Jennings and Steuart Smith, a status that I enjoyed because I could do a variety of gigs without any one producer being dependent on me. They would call John first, then Steuart, and if neither of them could do it, they'd think, "I guess Pete would be okay." After the jingle session, I would stop at the local community college to give a couple of lessons, and then head down to the docks in D.C. to board the paddle wheel boat. That was a lunchtime Dixieland banjo gig. I loved playing tenor banjo, especially in a band situation, delving into the Louis Armstrong repertoire. I had done a couple of gigs like that at Senator Ted Kennedy's house in McLean, Virginia, so I knew some tunes. The boat gig lasted for an entire summer, and it was great to be out on the water.

When the boat docked, I would jump in the car and drive across town to Ellsworth Studios for some more teaching, and then at 6:00 p.m. I would drive downtown to the National Theater, Ford's Theater, or the Kennedy Center to play a show with my tux on. After that, I would trade the tux for jeans and go down to Old Town Alexandria to play a rock and roll or jazz gig until 2:00 a.m. This multiple-gig schedule went on seven days a week. When I look at my calendars from back then, they are almost solid with black ink. However, it was still of the utmost importance to me to keep improving. After all the gigs, when I got home I would open Book #1, the old, original "fake book" with the melodies of hundreds of standard songs. I would read, playing them as solo pieces with chords and a bass line, until I fell asleep for a few hours. The guitar was never really out of my hands.

I played lots of shows with old school luminaries including Ginger Rogers, Joel Grey, Marvin Hamlisch, Jane Olivor, and the awesome Eartha Kitt. Each act was interesting in its own way. Ginger's guest backstage was Nancy Reagan, and they looked like two tiny birds fluttering about. Hamlisch was known to be tough on guitarists, but I did a couple of gigs with him that worked out fine. At one, when he was conducting the National Symphony, he was introducing his latest opus: the theme from the James Bond film, "The Spy Who Loved Me." The song was entitled "Nobody Does it Better." The main theme was introduced by the electric guitar. When the hundred-piece orchestra played a huge Bb chord, I closed my eyes and just bathed in the lush surround sound. Unfortunately, that's when I was supposed to be playing the main theme, so that got a tap on the conductor's music stand. Marvin let me slide on that one, though, and the next time around I played the right notes at the right time.

Jane Olivor brought her own drummer from Los Angeles for her Kennedy Center show. When I heard her call him "Cubby," I asked him if he was former Mouseketeer Cubby O'Brien, who used to play drums on the Talent Roundup portion of the *Mickey Mouse Club*. He was indeed, and he was still a terrific drummer, although he'd outgrown his mouse ears.

I did a few things with Eartha Kitt. I played in the pit at The National Theater for a run of "Timbuktu." The visual concept was a re-creation of the flamboyant "bird of paradise" costumes from the Cotton Club era. When Eartha would make her entrance, wearing a feathered headdress that almost grazed the raised curtain, the audience would go wild. When they finally stopped applauding, she would do her trademark growl, and they would go wild again. That happened every night, but it was at a different show, a one-nighter at the Warner Theater around the corner, where I saw Eartha do an actual showstopper. She did a very heavy number, flamenco style and mostly in Spanish, with me playing flourishes on the guitar. The song increased in intensity until the final chord. She was standing at the lip of the stage, almost in the audience, and the show stopped. The applause went on and on, almost hysterical, like the kids at a Beatles concert, and the crowd stood up. What started as a standing ovation turned into something resembling Holy Communion in a Catholic Mass. Row by row, the patrons filed into the aisles and made their way in an orderly line down to the stage, where each person kissed Eartha's hand before returning to their seat. Most of them were in tears. This spontaneous ritual took about twenty minutes, after which the show continued on.

I played a couple of shows with Bob Hope. Musicians loved him, because he always hired a dozen or so of us, just to keep everybody working. The gig consisted of playing the old melody, "Thanks for the Memories," while he walked from the wings out to the microphone. That took about ten seconds. Then you'd just sit and laugh at his jokes until he was done, at which point the band would play "Thanks for the Memories" for another ten seconds while he walked offstage. That was a great twenty-second gig!

I also did a show around that time with Frank Sinatra. Senator Hubert Humphrey, a beloved politician in Washington, was retiring. There was a big party thrown for him in the ballroom of the Washington Hilton, the same place where I had seen Hendrix a decade earlier. I played along with the orchestra for some dinner and dance music, and when the show started, Al Viola, Sinatra's guitarist, sat down next to me. For the rest of the gig, I had the option of following Al's charts without playing anything, or watching Sinatra, who was about ten feet in front of me. Of course I was looking at Sinatra's back, but that gave me the opportunity to see the audience reaction to his show, and react they did. At every gesture, whether he lit a cigarette, straightened his necktie, or took off his hat and threw it onto the piano, women in the audience screamed, and some of them simply collapsed on the floor. They weren't teenagers. They were wealthy middle aged women, successful on their own or as half of a power couple on Capitol Hill; but in this moment, they were teenagers again at the Paramount on Broadway, out of control, screaming and fainting. It was chaotic to see but it occurred to me that I was seeing what Sinatra had been seeing for a half-century.

Leonard Bernstein turned sixty years old around this time, and a gala was thrown for him at the Wolf Trap Filene Center, a beautiful national park for the performing arts nestled in the Virginia countryside. This was another show where some charts called for guitar, some didn't; I had time to sit and listen to the orchestra around me and watch Bernstein at work. His right-hand man, John Mauceri, did much of the conducting, and we all knew it was a "rise to the occasion" gig, because we were playing the maestro's music to an audience in which he himself was the honored guest. He was dynamic, hip, cool, and unpretentious, just the opposite of the image of a snooty composer. His music was challenging to play, and there was a sense that he was always on the edge, pushing things forward, for the orchestra and the listeners. It was also great people-watching to see his guests, including the entrancing Lauren Bacall, come and go. I felt honored to be there, and to spend not only the evening of the show, but also the rehearsal days leading up to it, playing, listening, and having the chance to watch and learn from one of the real greats.

I went down to Williamsburg, Virginia on occasion to play shows, including one with Tennessee Ernie Ford. When he sang "Sixteen Tons," it took me back to the little record changer on Oakland Street in Arlington, and at the end of the show, he gave his traditional sign-off, "Bless your pea-pickin' little hearts." I also played a show backing The Fifth Dimension down there. Although they were solidly mainstream, not funky soul singers, they sang and danced like real pros, and they did their renditions of a couple of great Laura Nyro songs.

I got a call to put a band together for a show backing Martha Reeves, who had numerous hits in the Sixties with "Martha and the Vandellas." This was my first time playing with a real Motown artist, reading actual Motown charts. We played "Dancin' in the Street," "Jimmy Mack," and so on. At the end of the night, she signed a photo for me: "To Pete. You thrilled my heart." Then she wrote my number on the "K" page in her address book, right after Eddie Kendricks of The Temptations.

I spent a lot of time in orchestra pits, playing *Evita* in D.C. and Pittsburgh, and loving the great noir-style charts for *42nd Street* at The National Theater. At one *Evita* rehearsal, the show's composer, Andrew Lloyd Weber, was giving the orchestra a few suggestions, and I noticed that he was wearing a button with one simple word: "Cats." I recall thinking to myself, "This fellow must really love cats." He hadn't yet announced the title of his next blockbuster musical! Not all the shows were big hits. I played one called *Forge of Freedom* at Ford's Theatre in 1976. It was a musical about Valley Forge. The producers evidently thought that men starving and freezing would make an evening of uplifting song and dance. *The Washington Post* review headline read, "Valley Forge Made Bleaker." It closed after a couple of shows.

There was another show, *Mara The Gypsy*, that ran for four days in the Terrace Theater in October 1985, upstairs at the Kennedy Center. It was a vanity project by a rich fellow who produced the show, directed it, wrote the music and the script, and unfortunately had no talent for any of those things. Of course, that meant he was a cruel dictator in rehearsal, constantly berating his amateur cast who, it was rumored, had paid him for the privilege of acting in this opus. He was not a musician, which didn't dissuade him from composing the score on a little plastic chord organ. He could press buttons to produce a few major and minor chords, so when the orchestrator copied out parts for us to play, the resultant sound was an orchestra sounding very much like a little plastic chord organ.

The show had other problems that became evident on opening night. The singers weren't actually able to sing on pitch, they couldn't remember melody lines, and they didn't know when to sing and when not to sing. The special effects were of particular concern. As the curtain rose on Act II on opening night, the leading actor was sitting in a garden reading the newspaper. The front page was clearly visible to the audience. It was woefully obvious that it was that day's *Washington Post*, not the Paris news from 1944, so the scene started with an unintentional laugh. Then the script called for a Nazi to burst in and fire a stage prop Luger pistol at the leading lady's head. According to sensible union rules, stage guns can't actually be fired, even with blanks. The sound of the gun report is done by a stagehand in the wings, carefully timed with the pull of the trigger. The ersatz Nazi followed the script to the letter, but when he pulled the trigger there was only silence, leaving the leading lady wondering if she was dead or not, and the Nazi wondering what to do next. The Nazi pulled the trigger again, to total silence. Someone must have nudged the stagehand, because at that point, the sound of the gun blasted through the speakers while the Nazi was shaking the phony gun in frustration.

The audience was in stitches, rolling in the aisles. The next night was even better, because after three tries, the Nazi, in a burst of improvisatory inspiration, threw the gun down on the floor and started strangling the lady. At that point, of course, the stagehand fired the offstage gun.

The finale of the show was clumsily lifted from *Evita*. While the orchestra played a solemn dirge, indistinguishable from the dirges that comprised the rest of the score, actors playing pallbearers carried the casket of the leading lady down the center aisle and up a set of stairs to the stage. During rehearsal, the producer saved casket rental money by using a foam beer cooler for this tragic scene. The first time the actors toted the real casket was on opening night, and they could barely lift it, much less carry it all the way down the aisle without dropping it a couple of times. When they got to the stairs, they were falling down on one knee, and hanging precariously over the orchestra pit. The audience was rolling in the aisles as the house manager mercifully turned up the lights. I packed up my gear, knowing there wouldn't be a next show!

I picked up a one-off gig at a resort on the island of Eleuthera in the Bahamas. As the big Boeing jet from New York City circled Nassau airport, I noted with interest a vintage World War II era troop plane, and I wondered if the old bird still flew. We landed, and I was adjusting to the heat as I boarded a golf cart to be transported to the plane that connected onward to Eleuthera. Of course, that turned out to be the ramshackle WWII aircraft! With no cabin pressurization, we flew low over the water, and through the long-warped seams between the metal fuselage plates, I could see oil streaming from the old Rolls Royce engines. I made up my mind to look for an alternative flight back to the mainland.

After my gig duties were done, I checked the map and found another airstrip, further north on the long, thin island. I got a cab, which in Eleuthera meant a great old '57 Chevy, and we wove through the narrow lanes of the "real" island, away from the resorts. The driver stopped at a tin roof shack. Inside was an unmanned ticket counter and a cooler stocked with Red Stripe beer. A few Rastafarians were lounging in the breeze that crept in under the tin roof. I asked them what the schedule was for flights to Florida, and when they stopped laughing several minutes later, one of the Rastas said, "There is no schedule, mon. Plane soon come. He will take you to Florida."

I lounged around the shed with the Rastas for an hour or so, when a tiny Piper Cub taxied down the single airstrip. Sacks were unloaded, and other sacks were tossed on board. I didn't inquire as to the contents of the sacks. The pilot signaled for me to take the co-pilot's seat. In that size plane, weight has to be balanced. We roared off and headed straight into a thunderstorm. Quickly, visibility through the front windscreen went down to zero as we plowed through dense clouds, creating the weird sensation of not moving at all. I gave up looking outside and turned my gaze to the instrument panel. The fuel gauge in front of me was ominously close to "E" and dropping fast. It was obvious that it would get there before we reached the mainland.

Sure enough, we ran out of fuel and the plane started coughing and bucking, getting ready to stall. The pilot was unfazed. "Now we switch fuel tanks." To me, that seemed like something more likely done while the plane was on the ground, but I wasn't going to argue the point. Still in the dense cloudbank, he cut the ignition and the craft went quiet, starting to descend toward the Atlantic. When the prop ceased turning, the pilot calmly threw the reserve fuel tank switch, and then the ignition. The prop sprang back to life and he leaned back on the stick to bring us up to our flight path, no doubt to the disappointment of the sharks below. An hour later we started descending again when, with minimal instruments, the pilot sensed that we would come out of the storm cloud directly over the approach to Fort Lauderdale airport. Having eschewed my original flight back to New York through Nassau, I rented a car and headed straight north. Route 95 never seemed so comforting!

First grade at Saint Thomas
More Parochial School, already
displaying sartorial splendor.

1963, pre-Beatles on *Ed
Sullivan.*

1964, post-Beatles on *Ed
Sullivan.*

At the Washington Monument, 1987. I played that 1965 Fender Stratocaster for a couple of decades, having paid $150 for it in 1971.

TRUMPET VINE   B
ACROSS THE DIVIDE   A
SEPT SONG   F#
SHININ   B
LEGEND   G
GREEN EYES   C#m
LIKE A RIVER   G
TAGA WAYWALTZ the of my... A G
LOVE STILL REMAINS   B♭/C

I learned Kate Wolf's great songs in real time at this first gig, playing them live onstage at the Birchmere.

With the Ramirez nylon-string, backing mandolin titan Jethro Burns at the Birchmere circa 1983. Guitarist Al Petteway's left hand is at the far right.

I played one G chord on my new Martin guitar and Doc Watson proclaimed it a "good sounding D-28." Of course he grabbed it and played a few licks. *Photo by Mary Beth Aungier.*

Bound for Glory was a great time…a fun-loving gang playing loud, original rock songs. We were on a bill here at the Birchmere with Steve Earle and The Dukes. *Photo by Mary Beth Aungier.*

Chasing Danny Gatton around the upper reaches of the fretboard.
Copyright 1980-2018 Dave Fimbres: SemiCharmedLife Photography LLC.
All Rights Reserved.

Bound for Glory plus Danny Gatton, playing a concert to support longtime progressive DJ Damian Einstein,1989.

Chapter 7: *Guitars Galore*

〜〜〜〜〜〜〜〜〜〜〜〜〜〜〜〜〜〜〜〜

I was starting to feel the urge to get back to some real roots music when I got a call from my longtime buddy Tom Principato, the blues enthusiast who had upgraded The Flying Hospital back in my high school years. His jump R&B band, Powerhouse, was going on sabbatical. He suggested that he and I do an instrumental electric guitar duo, along the lines of Chester and Lester, the great album that Chet Atkins and Les Paul had done together. As part of our preparation, Tom and I traveled up to New York to see a live Chester and Lester gig at The Bottom Line. Les goofed around, detuning and unplugging Chet's guitar mid-song, and he had a habit of following a tricky lick by shouting "Take that, Jeff Beck!" Jeff was not in the audience, so it was a strictly rhetorical statement. Armed with inspiration and a few stolen licks, Tom and I put our act together.

We started doing guitar duo gigs in the clubs around D.C. We were a perfect opening act, because with just two Fender amps, we could set up and tear down in no time. As luck would have it, Danny Gatton was putting together his dream band, The Redneck Jazz Explosion, at the same time. When they were booked for multiple nights at the Cellar Door, modestly billed as "Guitar Genius" shows, our duo was the opening act, sometimes joined by bass ace Steve Wolf. It was great playing to an audience of total guitar fans, who didn't expect us to sing or tell jokes. They just liked guitar, and they knew the history and the styles. One particular night was a bit intimidating, though, when Gatton, Buddy Emmons, and Lenny Breau all came downstairs and sat across the front row. If you ever went to the Cellar Door, you'll recall that the front row was about eight inches from the stage. I can safely say that I've never felt intimidated in any guitar situation after that set!

Upstairs at the Cellar Door backstage area, I ran into Dobro great Mike Auldridge from the Seldom Scene, and we hit it off right away. We were both interested in playing swing music with laid-back eighth-note grooves, as opposed to the intense tempos that were Gatton's natural feel.

Mike and I started playing a lot in his basement while he worked on mastering the pedal steel. He invented an eight-string Dobro to facilitate playing swing jazz chords, and after some songwriting and arranging, we cut the album, "Eight String Swing." It seemed logical to do some live gigs, so we took one night a week at the Birchmere, using the name "Front Porch Swing." We needed vocals to cover a full night, so I contacted Mike Stein, who did a lot of bluegrass and western swing gigs around D.C. Gatton had quit playing, discouraged perhaps, by the record industry's lack of understanding of his Redneck Jazz project. I wanted to help revive his interest in music, and I wanted to get him feeling comfortable playing the Birchmere, because I thought it could become a simpatico home base for him. He thought the club was too bluegrass and they were nervous that he might be too rock. I knew that once he met Gary Oelze, the owner, they would become best buddies, because musically, they were kindred spirits.

Danny didn't want to be a guitar star at the moment, so I talked him into playing bass in Front Porch Swing. My hope was that he'd be thinking, "I can play guitar better than Kennedy!" while I was fronting the band, and that would lead him back to the Telecaster. After a few gigs, he stopped showing up, as I expected. He started hitting a few licks in his garage, and he came back on his own stronger than ever. I was glad I could do a small favor for him with the Birchmere, since I certainly couldn't show him anything on guitar!

I continued to do music with Mike Auldridge, including a series of after-hours jams with the great Keith Whitley after the Birchmere doors were locked for the night. These would go on all night long, while Keith pulled out great honky-tonk songs by Lefty Frizzell, George Jones, and Merle Haggard. I learned a lot about real country music in those all-night jams with Keith.

Mike also booked me for a one-night Birchmere show backing pedal steel great Buddy Emmons. The Big E was the master of taste. It was a gig to lift you up to a higher level of musicianship, just to solo a bit and blend with his beautiful harmonies.

Another time, Mike called me up and said, "You should come over tonight. There's an eighteen-year-old banjo player downstairs, and I think you'd really like what he's doing." I went over and did, indeed, like what Béla Fleck was doing. We all went in the studio and cut a few things that have never come out.

One night after a Front Porch Swing gig, a woman approached me and said, "I should be in your band." This forthright proposal was my introduction to Cathy Fink. I soon learned that she knew western swing, country, folk, etc., better than the rest of us. The band morphed into "Rhythm Ranch" which was Cathy, Mike Stein, Bryan Smith on bass, and me, with the later addition of the multi-talented Marcy Marxer after she relocated to D.C. from the Midwest. We did lots of gigs, including a string of Birchmere shows backing classic country legend Patsy Montana, and a memorable night backing the dynamic Ola Belle Reed up in Pennsylvania. At the Spanish Ballroom in D.C., I learned how to play square dance rhythm from Cathy and Marcy. They soon embarked on a successful venture making kids' records for Rounder, so there was plenty of session work, too. They actually made one of my songs, "Air Guitar," a kids' music hit in the US, while a duo called The Singing Kettle made it a kids' hit in the UK. I continued switching from union chart-reading guy to roots music all-purpose guy, and I enjoyed the bohemian atmosphere of clubs and coffeehouses where jeans and tee shirts replaced tuxedos.

As the 1970s wound to a close, the cycle of roots music that didn't pay the bills versus union gigs that did came full circle again. I took a job as guitarist and band leader for a revival of *Godspell*. It ran for nine months at Ford's Theater. By the time the show closed, I had made a decent amount of money in a short span of time, and like any young musician, I figured that the next step was to spend it all in an even shorter span of time. My grail quest for the elusive roots music gig that actually paid the bills was still ongoing. I bought a Dodge van, had road cases made for my instruments, gave notice at my apartment, and headed west into the sunset, toward the promised land of California.

Chapter 8: Freelancing Coast to Coast

Just as the 1960s had ended with my longest road trip to date, from D.C. to Boston, the 1970s ended with an even longer one, from D.C. all the way to Los Angeles. I was an avid reader of a magazine called *Guitar Player*, and it was constantly extolling the virtues of living and working in California. I had played hundreds of gigs, but almost all of them were within a hundred miles of the US Capitol and I wanted to see the rest of the country. That said, I missed a lot of it on the way over because I was in such a hurry. I blasted straight through Virginia and across Tennessee, and I barely took notice of Arkansas and Oklahoma.

When I hit the Texas panhandle, I stopped for gas at a lonely outpost along the highway. There was an elderly fellow lounging in front of the station. I asked him if it got cold there in the winter. "Son," he said, "in the winter, there ain't nothin' between here and the North Pole but a barbed wire fence."

Once in Los Angeles, with no job and no connections, expectation was quickly replaced by reality. I lived in a cheap motel for a while, until I found digs at an apartment that was virtually identical to the cheap motel, only cheaper, because I paid by the month. It was located a couple of blocks behind Nudie's Rodeo Wear, and I would sometimes go in and ogle the sartorial artwork of Nudie and his right-hand man, Manuel. After a few auditions, I started getting some basic work playing weddings and cocktail lounges, although I was advised that I should "smile more." I'd never really thought about that. I went down to the Local 47 union hall and got my card and I signed on to Arlyn's message service. Every studio had a bank of telephones in the lobby, and on breaks the musicians would all call Arlyn's to find out where their next session was. I enjoyed the friendly switchboard voice as she would intone, "Nothing today."

Once I was in the Los Angeles union, I had the phone directory, so I cold-called some of the session guitarists. I introduced myself as a guy who had done a bit of session work back East. Most of them were very friendly. James Burton chatted for a while, telling me he had just cut some songs with Lionel Ritchie. He said, "That's some good country music." I noted with interest that he considered the rhythm and blues icon to be a country artist. I wasn't going to argue with James Burton about what was and wasn't country.

I hung up from my chat with James and dialed Tommy Tedesco. He was the dean of all L.A. session guitarists, and one of the pillars of The Wrecking Crew—the top studio players. He answered the phone. Session players always answered the phone, because that's where their work was generated. I gave him my quick spiel. Without missing a beat, he said, "TTG Studios, Wednesday, 10:00 a.m. See you there." On Wednesday, I was there on time. Tommy put a folding chair next to his and I sat and watched as he played his parts. A full orchestra was cutting a TV soundtrack for a detective show called "Hart to Hart." On the break, Tommy called the conductor over. "Nelson, this is Pete. Pete, this is Nelson Riddle." I kept my cool as I shook hands with one of the legendary arrangers in Los Angeles. I looked around, saw Shelly Manne on drums, and realized that the band was made up of jazz legends. Tedesco was as nice as could be, in a gruff uncle way. A couple of weeks later, he was playing at a jazz club near where I lived out in the Valley, and I chatted with him on the break. He asked me what gigs I was doing. I looked at the floor sheepishly and said, "Oh, mostly just weddings." Tedesco went into his gruff uncle mode. "Look," he said sternly, "any gig where you have a guitar in your hands is a good gig!" That bit of advice has stuck with me ever since. He was a good guy and a heck of a musician.

My next cold call was to Jimmy Stewart, a veteran session guitarist. Drawing on a reservoir of innate resolve, he had practiced a long and successful career in Hollywood despite the looming presence of an infinitely more famous Jimmy Stewart, the actor. Guitarist Jimmy Stewart told me to come right over to his house in Silverlake. He had a gig coming up at Donte's, a famous jazz club that was well known as a jazz guitar haven. We rehearsed a little bit and everything was cool. He would go into spacey dream sequences at certain points in the conversation, but that didn't bother me a bit.

We played the show; I met the other band members on the bandstand. David Benoit played piano, and an older man named Earl was on drums. As we started playing, Earl turned out to be a powerhouse. He would sometimes hit the snare with a crack that could be heard in Pasadena. We took a break, and I shook his hand. "You sound great, Earl! Do you ever play any R&B?" Earl looked down with infinite kindness at this little white suburban kid and said, "Well, I played on all of Little Richard's hits, 'Willie and the Hand Jive,' and 'You've Lost That Lovin' Feelin'." I realized that I was talking to Earl Palmer, one of the original inventors of rock and roll drumming!

I did some guitar duo gigs with Jimmy. At one of them, we were playing in a little Italian restaurant up at the top of Laurel Canyon. The music must have been enticing because during one of our songs, a coyote ambled into the club, listened for a little while, then turned around and calmly made his exit.

I made a point of going to hear the top L.A. session players whenever they did a club gig. They played in a very smooth, laid-back way that never broke a sweat. I found myself really missing the intensity and funk of New York City and the rusty-string D.C. Telecasters of Gatton and Buchanan. I wanted to get back

East. I sold my van and just about everything else I owned, and bought a ticket on a big old jet airliner. I was headed home.

When I got back to D.C., the first person I called was Gatton. I had a line on a dance at a fire hall, out in the country town of Nokesville, Virginia. That was exactly the kind of gig I wanted to play after the hushed, smooth jazz lounges in the hills of Los Angeles: a good old fire hall. I called one of my favorite D.C. rhythm sections, Rico Petrocelli and Robbie Magruder, so the gig turned into kind of a welcome home party for myself. It was a dinner dance for the members of a service organization. It might have been the American Legion. The members dined, then were getting ready to dance when the fellow in charge, who wore an officer's uniform with lots of insignia, silenced the room by banging a gavel on the table next to his dinner plate. "Welcome one and all to the annual dance! We are going to have a fine country band." He gestured toward the stage, where we were plugged in and ready to play. "But first, we will recite the Pledge of Allegiance to the flag." He paused for a beat. "Seein' as how we don't have a flag, if y'all could turn and face the Pepsi machine, we will recite the pledge." And that's exactly what they did. Danny and I exchanged furtive glances, Robbie assumed a poker face, and Rico's eyebrows went up to the ceiling. I had to admit that the Pepsi logo was indeed red, white, and blue. We segued directly into "Hey Good Lookin'." I was with my long-time buddies, and no one had to tell me I should smile more.

Before I left Los Angeles, I had gotten a call from Martha Reeves. She wanted me to put the band together for a few gigs in what jazz musicians called "the neighborhood": New York, Philadelphia, and D.C.

The first Martha Reeves gig was at The Peppermint Lounge in New York City. It was mainly an all-night dance club, the home of the "Peppermint Twist," but they would sometimes stop the disc jockey thing for an hour while a live act played. The hour that they booked for Martha and the Vandellas started at

2:30 a.m. The sun was up by the time we came up out of the Holland Tunnel, headed for the Philly show. That second gig was a bit bleary-eyed.

The third night, at the Carter Barron Amphitheatre in D.C., was a double bill with Motown saxophone ace Junior Walker and his band, The All Stars. If I was looking for funk, this was it. The All Stars went on first. It was a balmy night under the stars in Rock Creek Park, and I stood in the wings to watch the first act. They did an interesting bit of stagecraft. The band went on without Junior, and they started vamping on the groove of his infectiously funky hit, "Shotgun." As they played, I realized that Junior had come out of the dressing room and was standing right next to me, out of sight of the audience. He started wailing on the sax, playing great stuttering Texas-style riffs and Gospel phrases. His solo built and built, but no one in the audience heard it or saw him. As he reached a climactic point of funkiness, he strode out to center stage and massacred the crowd, starting literally on a high note. He had them. Martha was rested and in good voice, and our part of the show came off without a hitch.

I spent the rest of the year gainfully employed in the orchestra pit for *Zorba* at the Kennedy Center. Anthony Quinn, aka "Quinn the Eskimo," played the lead. He was larger than life. I loved hearing him deliver his dialogue. There were two bouzoukis required in the score; they wisely brought two real Greek players down from New York. They sat in the pit, right under center stage, facing the audience. We all had music stands, of course, but the Greek fellows didn't read music; they didn't need to. They had Greek girlie magazines on their music stands, unseen by the audience, but probably visible to Quinn, perhaps as a source of inspiration for his ribald character.

After one of the *Zorba* shows, I walked out of the pit into the backstage complex and almost ran into Michael Jackson. It would have been impossible to actually run into him because he was surrounded by a phalanx of beefy security guards. The Kennedy

Center has an underground entrance and a maze of tunnels, one of which leads to a secret elevator that can transport the president and his family to a private box at the center of the balcony, invisible to the rest of the audience. Jackson, a friend of Quinn's, was availing himself of the secret box in the absence of the president. As the King of Pop, he counted as royalty.

For D.C. musicians, presidential inaugurations were times when we put aside political differences, because, well, we needed the money. On the swearing-in day, it was not unusual to play three, four, or more gigs, driving around town in heavy traffic, avoiding the parade route, etc. Ronald Reagan's second inaugural was one such day for me. I started out in the morning rehearsing at the Hilton Ballroom with a soulful Texan, Freddy Fender. He was headlining an event later that night billed as "The Hispanic Ball."

I was glad to play with Freddy. He skipped past his country hits and went straight to swamp pop and Louisiana style rhythm and blues. After rehearsal, I put on my tux and beat it over to the Old Post Office building, a fancy upscale mall downtown. I had two gigs there in the afternoon. As soon as I arrived, I grabbed my 1920s vintage tenor banjo and became the strolling banjo guy (spreading good cheer everywhere I went, no doubt). At one point, I was strumming away near President Reagan, Reverend Jimmy Lee Swaggart, and the enigmatic Reverend Sun Myung Moon. They were getting ready to pose for a photo. At the last moment, the photographer shouted, "Get the banjo guy in there!" I was shunted into the picture by Secret Service operatives. No, I don't have a print of it, and yes, I wish I did have one because it was a trifle surreal.

I packed up quickly and headed back to the gig with Freddy Fender.

I did a few more shows with President Reagan, including a couple of the White House Correspondents Dinners, which were nicknamed "The Gridiron Club." They were a Hollywood style roast, with everyone, including the president, doing standup comedy routines. These events were top secret at the time, although they became a glitzy, and controversial, TV gala in later years.

Chapter 9: *Elton to the Rescue*

I received a call from the Kennedy Center to play in the house orchestra for "That's What Friends are For." It was an AIDS bene-fit TV special to be hosted by Dionne Warwick, with rehearsal the day of the show. On a freelance variety show, you play for any artist who needs a guitarist. They bring the charts with them from New York or Hollywood, so you don't see any music beforehand. It's a lot of work, but it can prove to be an interesting day. I showed up at noon, with my tux in the car, since there wouldn't be any time to go home between rehearsal and show time. I parked underground at the Watergate, walked across the street to the unmarked stage door of the concert hall, and made my way through the labyrinth to the stage. A pile of guitar charts lay on a chair near the drum-mer. I plugged in my amp and tuned up just in time for the first act downbeat. It was Mary Wilson, one of the original Supremes. Her songs came off without a hitch, so we moved on to the next act. It was Gladys Knight. I was psyched when we pulled up the second chart, "Midnight Train to Georgia." Just to play that classic tune with Gladys was an honor. Next up was Barry Manilow. Unlike most of the acts that traveled with conductors who led the orches-tra, Barry not only played his own piano parts, but he conducted as well, while singing and entertaining the crowd. He knew his stuff. After Manilow had run through "Mandy," "Copacabana," and his other hits, the contractor called for a twenty-minute union break. Everybody got up for a stretch, and most of the band wandered downstairs to the backstage canteen for an infusion of coffee.

At the time, I was naturally awake and didn't drink coffee, so I decided to stay in my seat and look over the upcoming charts.

The union stagehands were on break, too, so I was the only person in the cavernous concert hall. A concert grand Steinway stood freshly tuned about fifteen feet to my right. I was checking out a tricky chord voicing when I noticed someone coming out from the wings. It was Dionne Warwick, wearing jeans and a sweatshirt. Behind her was Burt Bacharach. They were chatting casually. It occurred to me that they had gone through an acrimonious professional split years before, and supposedly hadn't done any work together in over a decade. I stopped playing, and tried to disappear behind my music stand.

Neither Dionne nor Burt noticed me. They walked over to the Steinway. Burt sat down and opened a big sheaf of charts. Dionne stood next to the piano, on the left hand side, and they began rehearsing: "Walk On By," "Do You Know the Way to San Jose," "I Say a Little Prayer," and "What the World Needs Now Is Love." They ran down the whole repertoire, Burt covering all the parts on the piano, and Dionne singing softly. She sang those songs in a way no one has surpassed since she did the definitive versions back in the mid 1960s. The chemistry was palpable. I was just a few feet away from a great composer and a great singer. Their alchemy created an aura that was visible as well as audible. I knew that later on, they would probably do these songs on stage with the full orchestra, but nothing would equal this moment. I kept quiet as a mouse, and when they were done, they walked off stage as the crew started rigging lights and cables.

Frank Sinatra was next on the rehearsal schedule, and his guitarist, Al Viola, always traveled with him, so I had a break. Frank, Jr. came out and sang his dad's parts, sounding exactly like the older Blue Eyes. The band, with a few New York ringers added, swung the Basie-style charts. After "The Lady is a Tramp," the contractor called a break until the downbeat of the show, and the ushers opened the house.

Showtime came, and everybody was great. The gig was being shot for TV, and you might think that a production of this scale would be mapped out to the last detail, but there were still a few surprises in store.

I was hanging around backstage with Sinatra's band. Al, the guitarist, interrupted our chain of road stories with a wager. "I'll lay you ten-to-one odds that the old man doesn't go on."

"What do you mean, doesn't go on?"

"I mean he's not gonna go out on stage and sing."

"Al, it's a live TV telecast."

Al shrugged. "He's been doin' that sometimes, lately. He pays us all year 'round, and puts us up in the best hotels, but sometimes we fly out, and if he doesn't feel like his voice is up to par, we fly back home. I'll lay ya ten-to-one odds."

At that moment, Frank, Jr. appeared, negotiating his way through a maze of props and cables in the semi-dark backstage. "Pack it up, boys, the old man went home."

Al shrugged again, and winked at me. "I'm only sorry you boys didn't have time to lay your money down."

The show went on without the Chairman of the Board. When the full cast and orchestra assembled onstage for "That's What Friends are For," Stevie Wonder himself came out and played the little harmonica hook, and all the singers started trading licks on the ending vamp.

Things seemed to be wrapping up nicely when, without warning, a white stretch limo pulled up at the stage door and Elton John jumped out. He literally jumped, and ran directly onto the stage, grabbing the microphone just to the left of Stevie Wonder. Dionne Warwick, Luther Vandross, Gladys Knight, and the rest of the singers blended into a handclapping, vamping backup choir, while Elton and Stevie launched into a friendly duel. They were trading licks, pushing each other higher and higher. Needless to say, the audience went wild at the unexpected appearance of yet another bona fide legend, especially because Elton ratcheted his performance into high gear in a matter of seconds.

In the end, nobody was going to cut Stevie Wonder in a vocal riff contest, but the two of them managed to raise the whole building off the ground. Thinking back, though, the most memorable moment of the whole day was hearing Dionne Warwick softly singing "If you see me walkin' down the street" to her old compatriot Burt at the piano. That, indeed, is what friends are for.

Once again, I started tiring of the whirlwind of commercial gigs. I was the substitute guitarist for *Cats* at the National Theater. I played whenever the regular guitarist took time off. I would go in the stage door wearing jeans and a tee shirt, and take my place in a room in the back of the theater with some, but not all, of the band members. There were others in another room somewhere. Precisely at 8:05 p.m., a video screen would come to life, and the conductor, who I only saw on the screen, would start waving his baton. I never saw a "cat" or any other cast member in costume, and I never saw the show itself.

In between numbers, the musicians all picked up magazines and read idly until the last split second before the downbeat of the next piece. The whole experience struck me as a non-musical office job. I began to feel that if I was going to be cynical about it, I probably shouldn't be there. My old motto about how good it was to be the worst player in the orchestra was wearing thin now that I was a veteran, and I still suspected I might be the worst player in the pit. I decided to really commit to playing music that I loved. I felt that my long "session guy" experience would be beneficial in the world of roots music and singer-songwriters.

One of the last pit shows that I did was at the Kennedy Center with The Alvin Ailey Dance Theater. It was the world premiere of *Three Black Kings*, a symphonic ballet that Duke Ellington composed on his deathbed ten years earlier. He never heard it. The music was deep and great, and I thought back fourteen years to meeting Ellington in Boston. I figured he would approve of me getting out of the pit and following my dream onward.

Chapter 10: Roots

~~~~~~

I got a call from Gary Oelze, the owner of the Birchmere. "Do you want to play with Kate Wolf tonight?"

"Sure! Who is Kate Wolf?"

"Just come down to the club at four. Mike Auldridge will be there, and you guys can sort things out with Kate and her bass player, Bill Miller."

When I got to the club, there was already a line around the block. Kate had been getting airplay on regional acoustic music shows: Dick Cerri's "Music Americana" and Mary Cliff's and Lee Michael Demsey's influential programs.

The audience knew Kate's music much better than I did, but as soon as we started playing, there was a natural groove and texture that fell right into place. I enjoyed it a lot more than playing *Cats*. Kate's songwriting was full of compassion and had a sympathetic resonance with her listeners. Her voice was full and rich, with no histrionics, and it seemed to envelop the audience in a warm glow. I had seen Peter, Paul, and Mary do a powerhouse, high-energy acoustic show years before, but I had never seen the power of very quiet, slow music that was somehow invested with tremendous energy. Kate had that, and many people in the audience were crying deeply while her songs washed over them in a comforting way.

I did a few duo gigs with Kate, including a really nice show at the Star Theater in West Virginia. The stage was covered with flowers, and we played totally acoustic, with no microphones needed. I liked the music, the lyrics, the smart people in the audience, the acoustic sound, and the lack of any cynicism. These people loved what they were doing.

I started doing lots of backup gigs at the Birchmere, often-times for songwriters who just wanted to hear a little padding under their vocal. I learned, after Kate once asked me, "Can you play a little less while I'm singing?" to keep the song itself at the forefront, not the guitar part. I developed a secret technique. In backing a songwriter who played guitar chords, I would play something simple for an intro, and then not play anything at all when they started singing. At the turnaround between verses, I would play the same simple thing, and then stop playing again. While they were singing, and this seems obvious, I would look at them. I learned this from watching rehearsals for theater shows. Wherever the cast looks, the audience will look. When the singer was singing, I looked at her and listened with interest to the words of the song. If there was a solo I'd play it and then, you guessed it, stop again when they started singing. I found that by doing this, I was showing the singer and the audience how appreciative I was of the lyric. I avoided playing any competing melodic phrases that could throw the singer off of their pitch or phrasing. That simple reduction in the number of notes being played has been my approach to backing songwriters throughout my career. I've heard a lot of great songs, simply by listening instead of thinking about what I was going to play next!

Around the mid 1980s, Danny Gatton called me about playing second guitar and singing a little bit in his band. This was a sign to me that I had moved up a notch from follower to apprentice. I suppose it was based on something he said to Joe Kogok, a facile jazz guitarist who had worked with Danny. He said, "Pete Kennedy plays and sings pretty good, and he's not a pain in the ass." Of course, I considered that a high compliment! We got a steady gig on Wednesday nights at the Gentry, a club on Capitol Hill, and Danny quickly rebuilt his fan base. I would sing for a minute or two, followed by twenty minutes of wild guitar solos, another minute of singing, and the gig would go on like that. It was perfect for me, because I was playing my guitar and we were egging each other on. We never rehearsed or had a set list; we just got up there and played. John Previti was on bass, and Dave Elliott played drums. Sometimes Danny or Dave would get us all laughing so hard that the song would come to a halt until we were able to start up again. It was a fun gig. A fan of ours once told me, "I've seen Danny with several second guitarists, and you're my favorite, because you're not as good as him, but you don't care!" I got a good laugh out of that, and of course I agreed.

One night we were playing at Oliver's, a club out in Fairfax, Virginia. The first set was full of fire, and the second set was the opposite: a crazy extended medley that dissolved into TV themes and cartoon melodies. Near the end of the set, I saw Vince Gill come in the door with his gig bag. I knew he was playing right down the road at Wolf Trap that night. He was not famous yet, and no one recognized him. I'd seen him play out in California, so on the next break, I spoke with Gatton. "Vince Gill is here. You should let him sit in for a couple of tunes."

"Who's Vince Gill?"

"He's a Nashville Telecaster guy." Once Danny saw Vince's 1950s Tele, he was fine with it, if for no other reason than to hear what the guitar sounded like. Well, the third set was nothing like the second. Once Danny got the word that a hot licks Nashville guy was in the house, he went into overdrive. He played his hottest stuff, turned on the "genius button," and we closed the set with an "Orange Blossom Special" that was so fast I thought the club might spontaneously combust. Danny had a funny ability to be friendly and happy-go-lucky while at the same time mopping the floor with any other guitarist on stage with him. I was used to it, but I must say I give Vince a lot of credit for getting up for the encore after that third set. Of course, Danny mopped the floor with him, but Vince didn't seem rattled, and he got off a few good licks. They became good friends, and I've seen videos of them doing guitar stuff together down in Nashville.

The Everly Brothers, who my sister Chris and I used to imitate, reunited around this time. They had a great band that included Buddy Emmons on pedal steel and Albert Lee on guitar. I decided to try my "one-off lesson with a master" idea that had worked out so well with Joe Pass. I had figured out that if I asked for an individual lesson, the teacher would make fifty bucks. However, if I called around to my friends and organized a workshop, ten people would pay twenty bucks, and I had a better chance of convincing the artist to do it. I asked Albert after the Everlys' Wolf Trap show, and he agreed to come back in the morning for an hour. He was very gracious and cool. We started the hour by playing "Mystery Train" as a guitar duo. It seemed at the time that I was playing "Mystery Train" somewhere every day. Albert answered questions, borrowed a string bender Telecaster from my friend Bob Williams, and we closed out with a long duo version of Dave Edmunds' song, "Sweet Little Lisa."

There were a few master players that I felt too intimidated to approach. Roy Buchanan played in local clubs. I went to hear him, but he seemed like a serious grownup, not kid-like the way Gatton was, and I never met him. I felt like I would be interrupting his creative focus if I even said hello.

The Birchmere calls continued. Kate Wolf passed away out in California, but I used the lessons I had learned about acoustic dynamics from her when backing Bob Gibson, John Stewart, Tom Rush, and other songwriters. They were all interesting people who had been traveling the world for decades. I did a string of shows at the club as an adjunct member of Grazz Matazz. They were a progressive acoustic band featuring Al Petteway, who went on to become a famous fingerpicker.

Jethro Burns was the Django Reinhardt of the mandolin. He was known to "Hee Haw" watchers as a comedian, but he was known to mandolinists as, arguably, the best player who ever picked up the diminutive axe. Grazz Matazz backed him occasionally at the Birchmere, and he kept us in stitches with his one-liners while he blew us away with musical brilliance. He came in one day to Track Recorders to do a little playing on a Grazz Matazz album, and at the end of the session, he said, "Don't pay me what I'm worth, because I won't work that cheap!" That was the same session where Béla Fleck played a surprisingly musical solo using just the zipper on his parka. Béla was part of a loose, unofficial movement called the "New Acoustic," and I always found it a learning experience to play a few tunes with him or his colleagues Mike Marshall, Darol Anger, Tony Trischka, Jerry Douglas, Michael Manring, and Michael Hedges.

I dug that "New Acoustic" movement, mostly young blue-grass players who respected the tradition but sought to push the music forward. I saw the David Grisman Quintet at the Cellar Door, featuring guitar ace Tony Rice. I got to know Tony a few years later, when he was living in D.C. for a while and we were both part of the Birchmere "family." That meant that any night we weren't gigging somewhere, we were at the club for whatever show was happening. After hours, when the doors were locked, the "family" would sit around a table and shoot the breeze, some-times until daylight. The best bit of advice that Tony gave me back then was, "Pete, always remember that you're never more than one fret away from a right note!"

Tony came in to Bias Studios and played some beautiful stuff on a few of my songs, including "Shearwater." I played my old Ramirez classical guitar, so the tone would be distinct from his Martin D-28. Tony loved the Ramirez; he borrowed it to send to Santa Cruz Guitars so that they could make a copy for him. The luthier called me and said, "Your Ramirez has a lot of cracks in the wood. Do you want me to fix them?" I said "No! It sounds great, so just leave the cracks!" He laughed and said he figured I would say that.

I continued taking the backup gigs at the Birchmere, and I also started doing a few solo opening sets there. These were gui-tar-oriented shows featuring Leo Kottke, Doc Watson, Nils Lofgren, or the Desert Rose Band with the fantastic John Jorgenson on Telecaster. These players gave me the motivation to work up a solo set.

One of my solo gigs was at a Kennedy Center folk festival. When I got done with my side stage set, I wandered into the big concert hall. David Bromberg was playing some great blues, bluegrass, and funky gospel. Some of the other performers on the bill were gathering around him, singing improvised secular sanctified riffs. In the folk festival spirit, I jumped up with them and joined in. Afterwards we all hung out, exchanging "gigs from hell" stories.

A few weeks later I got a call from Bromberg's road manager, Jim Hale. "David's doing a benefit show in Kennedyville, out on the Eastern Shore. He wants to know if you want to come along and play some." Of course I did, especially considering the name of the town! I played a couple of solo blues things; I then sat in with Bromberg and his band for several tunes, most notably an extended version of my standard warhorse, "Mystery Train." I did a long solo and pulled out every lick I could think of. After the show, while we were all relaxing, David gave me his evaluation.

"Your solo started out great and it was going fine, then you lost them." My smile receded a bit.

"I lost them?"

"Yeah, with the Coltrane stuff. You didn't read the audience. You can play for *them* or you can play for *yourself*, but balancing those two things is the trick if you're supposed to be entertaining the crowd, get it?"

I got it. I wasn't insulted at all. I realized at once that Bromberg really cared about music, he knew what was good, and he also knew how to make it connect with the crowd. He always introduces his audience to deeper roots music than what they know when they sit down, but he does it in such an entertaining way that they never feel like they're being lectured. It was a great lesson for a player who was following in David's footsteps from sideman to an individual identity.

I did some freelance gigs down at The Twist & Shout in Bethesda, Maryland, backing Hank Thompson and rockabilly basso-profundo Sleepy LaBeef. I did a few shows and recording gigs with the great Hazel Dickens. She would make time stand still with her truly chilling *a cappella* version of the southern gothic anthem, "Oh Death."

Session work continued steadily, including a number of inspiring albums with folk maven John McCutcheon. I was teaching lessons off and on at Northern Virginia Community College. The jazz band director organized a jazz guitar clinic, with Charlie Byrd and me teaching. I was excited just to meet Charlie. He turned out to be a great guy who loved to play guitar. He had a million stories going back to World War II, when he was in the first US Army division to liberate Paris. He told me, "I didn't care about that. I just wanted to see if Django Reinhardt was still alive!" Charlie went on to become one of the great jazz players and the first American Bossa Nova guitarist. We hit it off, and at the end of the workshop, we played some Ellington tunes together.

A few days later, Charlie's manager, Pete Lambros, called me.

"Charlie wants to start a band."

"Great! Brazilian music?"

"No. He wants to play some blues and just have fun." We played together a few times a month for years after that, usually at the King of France Tavern in Annapolis, Maryland. We also played the Birchmere, The Barns at Wolf Trap, and we opened for Gordon Lightfoot at the Merriweather Post Pavilion. One night, after our gig at the King of France, Charlie had already packed up his guitar when jazz legend Barney Kessell suddenly jumped onstage, plugged in, and counted off a blistering version of "Cherokee." I obligingly chimed in, and we traded some high velocity solos until the coda, at which point he unplugged and disappeared out the door, without so much as a hello or goodbye!

I always loved playing with just two guitars onstage, as I did not only with Charlie Byrd, but also with Tom Principato, and a few times with Danny Gatton. There is a groove and a chemistry in two guitars conversing with one another. D.C. was a great guitar town during the period when Charlie Byrd, Tom Principato, Roy Buchanan, Danny Gatton, Al Petteway, Tony Rice, John Jennings, and Steuart Smith were all headquartered in town.

In the mid-1980s, I was playing an outdoor gig with Bob Margolin, who was working out of D.C. after a long career on the road with Muddy Waters. We were on a break when Bob suggested that we have a friend of his sit in. The guitarist had just arrived in town from London after working with Nick Lowe, and he had a cool old Fender. Bill Kirchen got up with us and sang a Chuck Berry song, "Let it Rock," and we became steadfast Telecaster buddies. I started doing some trio gigs around town, including a regular weekly gig at a biker bar in Virginia where I did one night and Bill took the next. I called my trio "Good Rockin' Tonite" in honor of the classic rockabilly tune.

Around that time, I was playing an interesting gig with the Rosslyn Mountain Boys, one of the original country-rock bands in D.C. Their topflight pedal steel player, Tommy Hannum, had left town to work road gigs out of Nashville. The Mountain Boys were stuck for a steel player, so they hired me to cover the pedal steel parts on my Stratocaster. That was a great learning experience and it had a big influence on my playing style, using the volume knob and bending strings in tune.

The Rosslyn Mountain Boys booked a gig high on a mountaintop, over a West Virginia coal mine, on a hot summer day. Steuart Smith and I drove out together. The coal miners and their families assembled on one side of a makeshift outdoor dance floor, and we set up on the other side. We opened with a Hank Williams song. They didn't dance. They didn't applaud either. We launched into a Johnny Cash song. The miner's faces, etched by the years down in the belly of the mountain, showed no reaction. They huddled together for a few minutes, and then one of them, their designated spokesman, stepped forward and addressed the band. "No offense intended," he spoke apologetically, "but don't y'all play anything by the Eurythmics?" We realized that MTV had come to the mountains.

I had done a string of double bills opening up for Nils Lofgren at the Birchmere and the 9:30 Club, with both of us playing acoustic and singing. I got a call from Nils on a Friday in June of 1984. He suggested that we get together and trade some licks. We decided to hook up after the weekend. On Sunday, I had a gig with the Rosslyn Mountain Boys. Drummer Bob Berberich said, "Hey guys, guess who got a call on Saturday from Springsteen to head straight up to New Jersey, join his band, and tour for the rest of the year?"

I said, "Let me guess..."

On a crisp autumn night in 1985, there was a Rosslyn Mountain Boys gig at a barn out in the countryside. Steuart Smith, Nils, and I all set up our amps and pulled out our Stratocasters. Nils was on a short break from the "Born in the USA" tour. Joe Triplett and Peter Bonta from the Mountain Boys also had Strats. We all decided that five Stratocasters was a case of over-twang, so we put the electrics away and grabbed acoustics. Instead of playing an organized show, we all spent the the night sitting around the campfire, singing Beatles songs and eschewing guitar solos. No volume wars and no competition; just a lot of fun.

Chapter 11: Al Green's Blessing

It eventually occurred to me, since I was practically living in recording studios and starting to write my own songs, that I really ought to put out an album. That was a leap, because any subsequent critique, good or bad, would be about me, not about the artist I was backing. I reached back to my old freelance confidence training: just do it. I decided to bypass "sophomore slump" and release two albums at the same time.

When those first two records came out, I was invited by folk disc jockey Dick Cerri to play a showcase at the Birchmere. He had a big following of listeners, and they packed the club. I was getting more confident as a front man, and I even got offered a job as a stand-up comic. (I turned it down. I wasn't *that* confident.) After the show, I said hello to Mary Chapin Carpenter. She was very shy back then, going through the same process I was, becoming more confident about performing. I said "You've got great songs. When are you going to do an album?"

She looked down at the floor in a shy, sweet way, and said softly, "Oh, I'll never make an album."

Cathy Fink always had an album, a tour, workshops, etc., going on, and she was great at pushing her projects forward. In the spring of 1986 I got a call from Cathy. She asked if I would play guitar for her at her Nashville debut at the historic Exit Inn. She'd been studying hardcore country music, and she was expert enough to write her own songs that sounded like Loretta Lynn classics. More importantly, she shared Loretta's fearless lyrical take on women's issues, a risky and courageous stance in the macho country music world. That phone call was a dream come true for me. It was not only my first chance to play in Nashville, but also the opportunity to grab a guitar and a notebook and drive alone across the South, the source of so much music that I loved and sought to emulate. I accepted the gig, and finally, I was on the road.

I left D.C. for Nashville with the "Smithsonian Collection of Classic Country Music" box set on cassette. There was a mother lode of great music on it, and that was my soundtrack down through the Shenandoah Valley and across Tennessee. The show was packed; many of the patrons were younger generation journalists who were spearheading a return to the unvarnished honesty of earlier country music. I chatted with two of them after the show. Chris Skinker was delighted with Cathy's songs and sound. She sensed that we had really delved into the history of the music. Chris invited me to tour the archive of the Country Music Hall of Fame, an area not open to tourists, so we set up a time for the following day.

Next, I chatted with Jay Orr. He was a young newspaperman who was following, and supporting, the trend away from Top 40 commercialism. We set up a meeting time for the following day, so I was already busy in Nashville.

Chris showed me around the stacks of books, scholarly papers, magazines, concert programs, and thousands of 78 rpm records that comprised the archive. Then she showed me the *coup de grace*, the guitar vault. I sat down and she started pulling out cases. Included were the first Martin dreadnaught, made for the Ditson music shop in Boston; Les Paul's "log," the homemade solid body on which he recorded his hits; and guitars owned and played by Chet Atkins, Merle Travis, Hank Williams, and Gram Parsons. It was an unforgettable hour. I was starting to love life on the road.

At the *Nashville Banner* building, I sat down at Jay Orr's desk. He asked me, "When do you need to be back in D.C.?"

I told him I had left the upcoming week wide open. "Okay," he said. "I'm going to draw you a map." He traced my route from Nashville to Memphis, and showed me where to turn south on Highway 61. He kept up a running commentary. "You need to go to Graceland, the Sun Studio, and the old boarded-up Stax studio, then head south to the Crossroads of 61 and 49. You'll pass through the Parchman Prison Farm, then turn west across the Big Sunflower River toward Dockery Plantation and continue on to Indianola. Eventually you can get back on 61 and head down the river to Vicksburg, where you can find a motel room." As he reeled off the places, I mentally checked off the names that went with them: Elvis, Jerry Lee, Carl Perkins, Roy Orbison, Johnny Cash, Sam and Dave, Otis Redding, Al Green, Robert Johnson, Son House, Muddy Waters, BB King. I felt like I had just been given a treasure map.

The first stop on my southern odyssey was Memphis. I left Nashville in the afternoon, after spending a few hours at The Great Escape, a sprawling used record shop. I stocked up on cassettes for the road; supplement to the three hundred or so that occupied the passenger seat of my little Honda. The find of the day was a two volume set of the Hank Williams "Health and Happiness Hour" radio shows. Pure gold. As I traveled to Memphis on Highway 40, I had the perfect road music for a gypsy trip through the Deep South. I could pick up the legendary river road near Graceland, on the south side of Memphis, and head down into the heart of the Delta in the morning.

I headed first for Graceland, Elvis Presley's mansion. It was closed for the night, and for now, I was hungry. I searched Elvis Presley Boulevard in vain for some funky soul food. I finally settled on a somewhat less-than-funky Shoney's, where I could order a plate of shrimp and jot down some stuff in my journal over a cup of coffee. After I'd been sitting, absorbed in writing for a while, the waitress came over to refill my coffee cup. She leaned down, to talk softly. "Al Green's here." I looked up and she pointed across the room. The Reverend Green and another Roman-collared associate were seated in a booth with two classy looking women. The party was paying their tab and getting ready to go. I got up my courage and grabbed my notebook. "Reverend Green?" I nabbed them at the door. "Could I get an autograph?" It was only the second time in my life that I'd made that request, the first time being Duke Ellington in Boston fifteen years earlier.

He smiled that big Al Green smile, took my notebook and wrote in it, "Life and Peace, Al Green." Then he took my hands in his, looked up to the sky over Elvis Presley Boulevard, and sang "God bless you." He didn't say it. He sang it.

Blessed by Al Green in Memphis, I knew everything was going to be okay from then on. After my morning tour of the Graceland mansion, I was ready to turn south down Highway 61, and dive into the heart of rock and roll. I bore to the left at the crossroads of Highways 61 and 49.

Following 49 down into Sunflower County, I drove straight through the Parchman Prison Farm, the infamous "murderous home" referred to in blues songs. Driving through these acres, made rich with the blood of Africa, you begin to get a true sense of the blues.

A few miles below Parchman, I was just north of the junction at Ruleville. I intended to turn west, passing Dockery Plantation, to eventually rejoin Highway 61 and continue south. A bulletin came on the radio: "Tornado warning for Sunflower County, effective immediately. Get inside, now!" I was like the motherless child in a Blind Willie Johnson song: a long, long way from home. The nearest refuge was a place called Junior's Junk Shop. I pulled over and went in. The place was dimly lit, and as the greenish-grey tornado clouds rolled in, it got darker. I poked around among Junior's junk for a while. Junior and his grandson eyed me silently. We could all feel the drop in barometric pressure; the room was permeated with a tacit unease.

In a dusty vegetable crate, I found a stack of old Hank Williams 78s. Now I felt like I was really on a southern road trip. I handled them like talismans, turning them over carefully: "Lovesick Blues," "Mind Your Own Business." Thunder rolled outside. Junior made his way over to me, between the old wringer washers and butter churns.

"You like them old records?"

"I like Hank Williams."

"He was a great man."

"Yeah. I've been listening to some live tapes." My northern speech seemed painfully obvious, but Junior didn't mind. He had switched from a silent, mistrusting watcher to a gregarious Mississippi raconteur. With the tornado roaring outside, I wasn't planning on going anywhere for a while, and let Junior warm up to his subject.

"I met the man."

"You met Hank Williams?"

"Right here in Ruleville. I was no bigger than him." He pointed at his grandson. "Old Hank played a concert right over at the high school."

His eyes lit up with the memory, not only of the concert, but also of himself at the age of five or so, and of Ruleville: how small it was back then, how small it was now, still surrounded by the black dirt cotton fields and the swampy lowlands around the Big Sunflower river.

"After the concert, Hank stood at the door, and shook hands with every single person as they left. Then he climbed in a long black Cadillac and rode off."

We talked while the storm rumbled by. Like most of the people I encountered in the rural South, Junior liked the old country music better than the current crop, and he felt that something was lost when the new convenience store took over the corner lot at the single stoplight in town. I asked him about Dockery, the legendary farm where, it's said, Robert Johnson learned the blues at the feet of Son House. Junior had heard of the place but it didn't have any special resonance for him. In fact, it didn't seem that the blues, the art form that started as the local play-party music right in this neighborhood, was really a part of his world. But old Hank—meeting Hank was the event of his life.

The storm passed, and I climbed back in the car, ruminating about Junior. In this rural area, where only the cars seem changed from the 1930s, I was meeting two types of deep southerners. Some saw me as an outsider bumping up against a closed circle, which they tightened further to keep me out. Others recognized my strangeness and decided to initiate me (a little bit) into the folklore—not all the way in, by any means, but far enough to convince a northerner that Hank Williams was real, and he shook people's hands.

I took a right at the light and crossed the Big Sunflower. A little to the west, on the road to Clarksdale, stood Dockery Farms, according to a big painted barn overhung with Spanish moss. I pulled off in a grove of cottonwoods and just soaked up the vibe for a while. The path to the left led to the laborer's village, probably still much like the antebellum slave shack towns. That would mean that every morning at sunrise, the workers would cross the road right here, heading out to the big fields beyond the barn. What songs did they sing? I turned south on 61, toward New Orleans.

My first act in the Crescent City was to sleep in the car for a couple of hours. When I woke up, it was just getting dark. Time to explore. A radio somewhere was playing loud—Fats Domino, Lee Dorsey, The Meters. It wasn't an oldies vibe, either. It was the present-moment music of the street.

I walked down the "no man's land" in the middle of the road to the Carrollton Diner. Inside, the curvaceous counter was crowded, everyone eating massive waffles. The unofficial floor-show was the counter man, who kept up a running rap to a free-lance melody. I listened for a while, ate a waffle, and made my way back out to Carrollton Street. Here on this bend in the river, you could feel that you were at the heart of something. When you breathed in, the air was sweet with rhythm. I rode the streetcar back to the Quarter, next to an escape artist, who told me that his career began when he stepped out of the audience to volunteer for a trick and found out he was a natural. There were a lot of escape artists, in their own way, riding that streetcar.

After café au lait and beignets at the Café du Monde down in the French Market, it was time to find the car and head north. I wandered down the dim streets and past dark alleyways. I was parked near the old #1 cemetery, right across the street from Marie Laveau's place, where she practiced African magic. Voodoo. I crossed the long bridge and rolled on up through Alabama, past the big Birmingham steel mills, toward Virginia and home.

Heading back up north from my first solo southern swing, my head and notebook were filled with melodies, lyric ideas, snippets of conversation, and other ephemera of the road. As I crossed the border into Virginia, I decided to roll the roulette wheel for one more adventure. I knew that there was a spot on my map called "The Carter Family Fold." It piqued my curiosity. I decided to veer off the Interstate and explore the back roads around Bristol, in search of lore concerning the Carters, true pioneers of country music.

The Carter Family Fold turned out to be a community gathering place where weekly dances were held, celebrating the spirit of the deep folklore in these misty mountains. The Carter's homestead was nearby. Everything was shut down on this cloudy Thursday afternoon, so I stopped down the road at an old converted railroad depot. Inside, the walls were lined with guitars, fiddles, and banjos. A wood stove burned in the corner. The owner was cordially silent, until I took down a nice old D-28 and picked a little bit of "Black Mountain Rag." I'd figured out that traditional music was the *lingua franca* of the rural South, and the best way to break the ice. The owner warmed up right away, and we chatted.

"You from up north?"

"Yeah. Arlington. Northern Virginia, I guess."

"Son, you're a long way from home. Just travelin' around?"

"Yeah, that's about right."

"You play pretty good. What time you headin' out?"

I hadn't been on a schedule for weeks. "Oh, I don't know."

"You oughta stick around. Chester usually comes by on Thursdays, and he's always lookin' for someone to beat rhythm." I had no idea who Chester was, but I decided to wait.

Sure enough, a half an hour later, a beat-up Ford Econoline pulled into the lot. Three fellows got out and ambled into the shop. They looked to be in their sixties. Chester was obviously the alpha dog. He took a fiddle, an old Guarneri copy, down off the wall and rosined the bow. The shop owner spoke up.

"Chester, y'oughta let this kid beat some rhythm. He can pick."

Chester looked out the window, toward the Smokies in the distance. "Oh, I don't know." He was skeptical, and I decided to lay out for a while, hanging outside the circle. The chemistry of a jam session is not always as robust as it may seem, and I didn't want to upset the vibe.

Chester started playing. He was great. He reeled off "Devil's Dream," "Billy in the Lowground," and "Cross the Big Sandy." When he hit "Blackberry Blossom," one of the trickier tunes, I decided to jump in. There's a lot of leeway in the rhythm part, and I started feeding him some swing chords, then changed up and spun a daisy chain of old-time bass runs. He responded right away, matching each style with the appropriate fiddle voice, all the while spinning daring improvisations over the changes. At the end of "Blackberry Blossom," he simply scraped the bow right into "Salt Creek," and we were off. The other guys pulled fiddles down and joined in, so the solos got passed around. They played "Fisher's Hornpipe," "Cripple Creek," "Ragtime Annie," and "Maiden's Prayer." I lucked out. I knew all the tunes they played. There are thousands more that I didn't know, but while a thunderstorm blew outside, my luck held.

They stopped after every two or three tunes, settling back to tamp their pipe tobacco and tell yarns. No one mentioned the rain, nor was there any feeling that we'd be going anywhere soon. Chester told a few stories for my benefit, knowing the other guys had already heard them. He let on that he kept his fiddle on the wall at the depot because his family couldn't stand hearing the same old tunes. They all listened to the radio, that modern stuff, and the subtle play of filigree and four-string improvisation went right over their heads. Whenever Chester felt like playing and smoking his pipe, he came down to the depot.

During one break, he offered a little history. "My family has been in these hills since 1834. My great-granddaddy talked with a brogue."

He paused, reflectively. "Son, I wasn't born yesterday. I have been to Harper's Ferry. I've been around a few corners." He tamped his pipe. "I've been as far as Alaska."

"What were you doin' way up there?"

"Air Force. I was stationed there back around '58, '59. Keepin' the world safe from the Russians. I played this very same fiddle in the saloons up there. I got drunk one night in the Yukon with an opera singer on my lap, and I never missed a note!"

All the guys laughed uproariously, although they'd probably heard the story a hundred times. Chester turned thoughtful again.

"Y'know, I've got a boy about your age. He's a good boy, but he don't care about fiddlin'." He looked back out the window, toward the French Broad River, and the Smokies beyond. "I don't agree with a lot of the things his mother taught him, but I guess it's too late now." He lit the pipe. "There ain't too many kids your age care about this stuff, but I feel like it oughta be passed on, like it was passed down to me."

Chester sighed, gritted his teeth down on his pipe stem, and kicked off a furious version of "Black Mountain Rag." The three

fiddlers prodded each other, hitting fancy licks, trills, and trip-
let runs, in a game of raising the stakes, 'til Chester called "last
time," and they took it out. Laughing and shaking their heads,
they hung up their fiddles and bows and put on their coats. The
rain had stopped, but a cold front was blowing in. We could see
our breath vaporize as we fastened buttons on flannel overshirts
and denim jackets on the rickety porch. Chester clasped my hand.

"Son, you look a little tired and hungry. You gonna be alright?"

He was right about my road weariness, but I was buoyed up
by the music, and by a feeling that these foggy hills had spoken to
me through the thunder, and through these cantankerous fiddlers,
with their wild yarns and wilder improvisations. "I'll be okay."

We headed for our cars. As he climbed into the driver's seat
of the van, I called out to him. "Chester, is that a '71 or a '72
Econoline?"

He closed the door and rolled down the window. "A '72."
He lit his pipe again, shook the match out, and threw it on the
ground. "You know your vehicles, don't ya, son?"

I smiled and pulled the Honda out onto the two-lane blacktop, aiming once again for the Interstate. Thunder was rolling off
to the Northeast, somewhere over Wytheville and Galax, and I
was ready to go home.

Back in D.C., I couldn't wait to get the guitar warmed up
again. I had a feeling that all the southern culture I had absorbed
was going to bring about a sea change in my approach to roots
music. The journal I kept on the trip turned out to be the kick-
start to the world of songwriting.

By then—around 1985—it had sunk in that if I didn't write
a sheaf of songs and sing them, I would spend my career backing people who did do those things. After learning hundreds of
songs, I had an ingrained knowledge of form and structure, so it
wasn't hard to get started on a new album.

I wrote a song called "The Same Old Way" that was loosely
based on Tom Petty's style. To my surprise, it was played on the

regional alternative station, WHFS. I figured that, if I was going to get recognition as a songwriter, I'd better continue writing. I wrote "Distant Thunder" based on my journal notes from that rainy night drive through the Yazoo Delta, and a rockabilly raver called "Run Red Lights."

Having assembled a catalog, I put together a band, Bound For Glory, with the intention of doing all originals. They were seasoned veterans: drummer Pete Ragusa, on a break from The Nighthawks; Jon Carroll, session singer, guitarist, and keyboard monster; and Johnny Castle, bass player for one of my favorite bands, Switchblade. They all sang better than I did, but I was the bandleader and I wrote the songs, so I laid down the law. A glowing Washington Post review and a few Washington Area Music Awards (Wammies) followed, and we hooked up with Tom Carrico, one of the top talent managers in town. Tom booked us into the Birchmere as the opening act for Steve Earle and the Dukes on their first national tour. That was an epic show for me, because I had played there so many times as a backing musician.

I still did recording work for others, including a session with the Smith Sisters, Debi and Megan, at Bias Studios, with Jonathan Edwards producing. I was glad when the sisters started calling me for live gigs. One of the great perks of working with Debi and Megan was that they were close friends with Doc Watson. That meant traveling down to the mountains of North Carolina for the festival he had just started presenting as a memorial to his son Merle. The festival was small, just a few hundred patrons, but the music was the top echelon. All around the grounds, you could wander and hear Jerry Douglas, Sam Bush, Mark O'Connor, Tony Rice, David Grisman, Béla Fleck, and true giants like Bill Monroe, Earl Scruggs, and of course Doc himself. Everyone jammed together in a myriad of formations, and the best part was that the backstage was a hive of constant bluegrass and folk activity.

I spent part of an afternoon at Merlefest lazily playing rhythm while Tony Rice, David Grisman, and Jerry Douglas traded solos on modal jazz chord sequences. I was running over a cool descending chord pattern with Tony when the stage manager came backstage.

"Pete, we need somebody to fill in for fifteen minutes on the main stage. Can you get out there and plug in?"

The small crowds at the early MerleFests were great. Not only were they music fanatics, but most of them were guitar aficionados as well, so I pulled out all the stops. I closed with a breakneck version of "Orange Blossom Special," and the hot lick-loving crowd roared its approval. I walked off stage, feeling pretty good to have held my own in a rarified atmosphere.

I packed my guitar away and strolled into the catering room. Tony Rice, David Grisman, Sam Bush, and Flux, as Jerry Douglas was known in those days, were hovering around the buffet, noshing and trading stories drawn from their collective years on the road. Over in the corner sat Bill Monroe, the Father of Bluegrass. He was by himself, and I barely noticed him until I heard a small voice float above the crowd noise.

"Kennedy?" Three rising notes. It sounded like a mandolin riff. "Kennedy?" It was Monroe. He was calling me from across the room. I moved closer to make sure I heard the faint, high-pitched voice correctly. "Kennedy!" He softened his tone, seeing me draw near. "Kennedy, you've played here before, haven't you?"

I felt a flush of pride. Bill Monroe noticed my show.

"Yes, sir, I have played here before." Then I waited for a compliment, the approval of the master.

Monroe looked left, then right, in a conspiratorial way, and whispered to me, "Do you know where the men's room is at?"

I put my arm out and he took it, rising unsteadily from his chair, and I led him around to the bathroom door, waited 'til he was done, then got him back to his seat.

Looking around the backstage at my own generation of musicians who followed in Monroe's footsteps, it occurred to me that helping a frail, elderly man find the bathroom might actually be a higher calling than playing a fretted instrument really fast. When I told David Grisman about Monroe's aborted compliment, he just grinned. "Oh, he knew what he was doing. That's Bill. He likes to yank people's chains."

In its early, small days, MerleFest was not only a great festival, it was also a reunion of family and friends of Doc. He spent the whole weekend either backstage or onstage, with some kind of instrument in his hands at all times. In fact, you could sometimes squint and catch a glimpse of the fiery twenty-year-old Doc, back before the world beyond the Great Smokies knew about him.

One night at the Birchmere, I was opening for Doc, and I marked the occasion by purchasing a brand new Martin D-28. It was a limited edition, with a torch inlay on the headstock, in place of the traditional logo. Best of all, it was a cannon. I carried it into the club, went backstage, and pulled it out of the case. I strummed a single G chord, and Doc, sitting a few feet away, turned his head.

"Boy, that's a good sounding D-28."

I hadn't even said hello yet, much less told Doc that I had pulled out a D-28. Heck, it could have been a D-18, but Doc knew right away. He heard, I guess, the rich midrange of the rosewood versus the warm brightness of a D-18. Maybe he'd just heard and played so many D-28s that the sound was as familiar to him as sunlight is to the rest of us, or as obvious as the difference between red and blue.

I passed the guitar over to Doc, and he played the intro to the Chet Atkins classic, "Country Gentleman," the lick that goes E9 to E diminished and back, up on the 12th fret. Then he passed it over to Tony Rice, who played a short solo version of his own tune, "Manzanita," cocking his ear carefully to hear the details of that particular box.

Properly baptized, that guitar was my powerful voice for years, but it never sounded as sweet as when Doc played those three little chords, way up there on the 12th fret.

A year or so later, I was in Northampton, Massachusetts, opening up for Doc at the Iron Horse, a venue of some repute, tucked away on Center Street just off of Main. The dressing room is downstairs, a somewhat barebones basement, but a decent place to relax between sound check and show time. The austerity didn't matter to me, and it didn't seem to matter to Doc, either. His accompanist, Jack Lawrence, got called away to give a lesson, and he asked if I would sit with Doc for an hour. Of course I agreed, always eager to hang for a while with a man who was not only a legendary performer, but also a walking encyclopedia of roots guitar styles. I set about figuring a way to tap his knowledge.

I knew that Doc loved talking about guitars, almost as much as he loved playing them. I also knew that he was expert on classic country guitar, 1950s style. So I devised a plan. I took out my guitar and started casually singing the Ernest Tubb country classic, "Walkin' the Floor Over You." When I got to the solo, Doc stopped me halfway through. "Boy, you're playing it all wrong!" He reached down for the latches on his guitar case. "Let me show you how to do it." Bingo!

Doc got out his Gallagher, still in tune from sound check. "Now, Smitty was the first one to play that one. Billy Byrd and Leon Rhodes came later." He then proceeded to walk me through the history of Tubb's guitarists, showing me the rhythm part for the pivotal tunes, then demonstrating the differences in style by playing each original solo, note for note.

An hour later, the guitars were put away, and my head was spinning from the subtleties of country-swing guitar, as taught by a true master. Jack walked in the door and asked, "So what did you guys do?"

As if we had rehearsed it, Doc and I answered in unison, "Oh, nothin'!"

My next southern trip was prompted by a phone call from Lisa White, the music booker at the 9:30 Club in D.C. I played there off and on, solo and with various bands. In fact, on one occasion I played a show at Ford's Theater, got out of my tux and into jeans, walked out the back door of Ford's, across the alley, and into the back door of the 9:30, ten feet away. That's how close the two venues were, although usually much farther apart, musically!

Lisa called to ask me if I had ever heard of the South by Southwest conference. I hadn't. She described it as a very small event, under the mainstream radar, where real aficionados gathered in the early spring to savor the roots music, fantastic food, and laid-back vibe of Austin, Texas. One of the selling points was that the major labels either didn't know about it, or else they ignored it as insignificant. Their corporate absence put it on the cutting edge. She suggested that, if I could get myself down there, she could get me on a showcase. I was looking for a reason to head back down South; the only other time I had been to Texas was when I had the pedal to the metal back in 1980, heading out for the West Coast. Now I wanted to check out Austin. I said yes.

I was advised to call ahead and find a cheap motel room, unless I could afford to stay at the conference itself. Since I couldn't, I reserved a room at a Motel 6 on I-35, on the south side of town. When I got there after the long drive from D.C. (and having spent the previous night sleeping in the car at a rest stop in Arkansas), the desk clerk told me the room wasn't ready quite yet. No problem. I came back in an hour. The room still wasn't ready. When I came back for the third time, around 4:00 p.m., she said, "The police are still in there." I was learning a little bit about Texas.

The early South by Southwest conferences happened almost entirely in a single hotel on the south side of Town Lake. There was no big convention center yet, and the conference wouldn't have been large enough to need one, anyway. There was a hall in the hotel with booths representing various Texas musical entities, and there were smaller rooms where panel discussions took place during the day and small showcases went on late into the night. Some of the showcases were so small that they took place in actual hotel guest rooms. Most of the music was by Texas artists, or by artists brought in, like I was, by an arts organization in another city.

I saw Townes Van Zandt get a standing ovation from a crowd of about twenty listeners in the *middle* of a song. That's how good the song was. Later that day I saw Alejandro Escovedo do a concert in a hotel room for about ten people. Sunday night closed the event out with a dance party featuring Joe Ely and his band. During lulls in the action, there was everything else in Austin. Live music all day, and all night, barbecue and great Mexican food on every corner. March offered balmy breezes that made the East Coast seem like distant Siberia. After a chat with a happy-go-lucky Doug Sahm, I gave Peter Rowan a lift to his little hacienda in the hill country, and we stopped for Mexican food at the Rio Blanco Café. Everyone seemed to live cheaply in stucco cottages with no furniture, just Fender guitars and amps scattered about. Naturally, I wanted to move there!

On the way back home, I scheduled a couple of meetings in Nashville with folks I met at the showcase in Texas. I checked into the cheapo Twelve Oaks Motel. As a newcomer in town, I was impressed by the fact that the legendary Music Row, where so much history had taken place, was a leafy suburban neighborhood. Even the major labels had small single story buildings. It was all very comfortable. I was sauntering down 16th Avenue South when I saw a good friend, Mike Connelly from Cherry Lane Music in New York, coming my way. Mike introduced me to his two companions, Jim Rooney and Tom Paxton. They were both legends with long histories. I shook hands with Paxton, and he said, "A songwriter, eh? Let's see what you've got. Hampton Inn, 8:00 a.m." I had just been given my Nashville marching orders to write a song with Tom Paxton at the crack of dawn. I decided not to negotiate for a later time slot, and agreed to see

him there. That settled, Mike announced the agenda for the day.
I was now part of their troupe. "We're heading over to Cowboy
Jack Clement's house in Rooney's car."

Cowboy Jack was an authentic legend. He was the engineer
at Sun Studios in Memphis in the 1950s, cutting the classics with
Elvis, Carl Perkins, Jerry Lee Lewis and Johnny Cash. That
alone would make him one of the inventors of rock and roll, but
since then, he'd followed a career of total quirkiness interspersed
with brilliant hits. He was way larger than life, and soon, the four
of us were sitting around his desk in the home office where he
held court.

Once his audience was settled in, Jack leaned back in his chair
and regaled us with stories. His laconic Memphis drawl filled the
room like a musical instrument. At one point, he started fiddling
with the controls on an ancient reel-to-reel tape recorder. He
talked while he fiddled. "The fellows from U2 came into the Sun
Studio a few years back. They wanted to get the sound." As Jack
threaded tape through the playback head, it occurred to me that
he invented the rockabilly echo by running tape past two playback heads in the mid 1950s, perhaps on the same machine he
was now fiddling with. He continued telling the U2 story.

"They cut a Woody Guthrie song. Nice fellows, but I didn't
really dig the rhythm section, so after they left, I had my guys
come in and lay down drums and slap bass." Music came roaring
out of Jack's speakers. It was Bono singing "Jesus Christ" over a
pumping rockabilly groove. "I don't think anyone's ever heard
that," he intoned. "We do a lot of things around here just for
drill."

Jack's funny little sayings were actually pearls of wisdom if
you thought about them for a minute, and I began to see what a
real record producer was: someone who inspires. Jack handed us
each a copy of his tongue-in-cheek "rules for the studio," and we
departed. I felt like I had had an audience with the Pope of rock
and roll.

In the morning, I made it over to the Hampton Inn on time. Tom Paxton had already been out jogging, and he was ready to write. I was amazed to see that he had one of those little computers that could be folded up and carried around. You could even use it on your lap. In 1986, I had read about them, but never seen one. He used it like a typewriter to compose the song, while we traded off lines. It was done in fifteen minutes. He explained to me that he wrote a song every morning, and another one every evening. That was about seven hundred songs per year.

In the evening, I met up with Paxton again, this time at the Bluebird Café. Tom was from Oklahoma, and there was a reunion going on at the club that night, with writers from the Sooner State playing their songs. A young man got up whom I had seen at an open mic on my first trip to town. The previous time he had played a couple of songs at The Sutler, a bar connected to a bowling alley. Tonight at the Bluebird, he did a couple more, and my impression was the same. His voice didn't seem exceptional; after all, I had just been jamming over the past few years with Keith Whitley and Vince Gill, but he seemed to skirt that issue by fixing an unblinking gaze, accompanied by a toothy smile, on the audience. In the tiny Bluebird, he had a way of thrusting his head forward as if to stare directly at each person and dare them to look away. I couldn't remember the songs later, but with his aggressive energy and Cheshire-cat intensity, it looked to me that Garth Brooks would be able to handle a large audience, should success come his way.

I developed a routine where I would play on the weekends with Good Rockin' Tonight, my bar-band trio, then spend Sunday driving to Nashville. I would drive back on Thursday and do more gigs around the D.C. Beltway. I began to think of the Twelve Oaks Motel as a second home. I soon learned that the Nashville scene was really all about hanging out and being a nice guy, not banging on the door of success. There was a pressure cooker of writers and producers who made up a tight clique on the inside of the money machine, but outside of that rarified space, the city was populated with talented people who pretty much ignored the charts and just did good work. Emmylou Harris had moved to town from California, and no one wanted to do anything jive while she was around. Steve Earle was also leading the pack of writers who were pushing hard for the honesty thing. The city sponsored a festival called "Summer Lights," and in one of my first full weeks in Nashville, I saw Rosanne Cash, Foster and Lloyd, The Desert Rose Band, The Sweethearts of the Rodeo, Webb Wilder, Marty Stuart, and Los Straightjackets, all one after another on the outdoor stage. Nashville was full of positive energy, balmy weather, and great new music.

I ran into Steve Earle in the parking lot of Shoney's motel. That's where bands met up to climb on the tour bus and take off on the road. He and the Dukes were playing a one-off gig in Kentucky, riding up and back on the same day, so I rode along. The band members, including a Telecaster buddy from Virginia, Michael McAdam, all retired to their bunks, and I sat up in the front lounge, chatting with Steve and L.A. songwriter Peter Case. I decided that trading stories and music trivia on a tour bus was my idea of a good time.

Hanging around in Nashville, I picked up a gig backing songwriter Fred Koller at a benefit show on Music Row for the Kerrville Folk Festival, an annual event held down in the hill country outside of Austin. Fred was a good guy who owned a used bookshop when he wasn't writing hit songs, so if you got tired of trading music trivia, you could trade book trivia with him. I liked backing him up on the guitar while he intoned in a voice filled with Louis Armstrong charm. I got my guitar tuned up, and wandered backstage.

The light was dim in the backstage room. The air was smoky. It took a few minutes for my eyes and ears to adjust from the bustle out in the club, but as I settled in, I realized that a jam was already in progress, and the air was crackling with electricity.

Guy Clark was weaving and bobbing like a shortstop with vertigo, lunging back and forth in the general direction of Butch Hancock, who complimented Guy's choreography with his own bob-and-weave. Seated on a tattered couch was Townes Van Zandt, who seemed to be the ringleader. They were all bashing out the blues in E on their guitars, and I realized in short order that they were making up a song, while they beat on their Martins and Gibsons between quaffs of a community bottle of whiskey. The music was wild, and the lyrics sounded like a resurrection of Blind Lemon Jefferson. Townes was wailing about women down on the Mexican border, and Butch was spinning his West Texas wordplay in between.

I could play the blues in E, so I grabbed my guitar and got in a few fills before the song trailed off and they turned their attention back to the whiskey bottle. It occurred to me that they could write a song on the spur of *any* moment, and, in fact, that particular song would never be sung again outside of that dressing room. It was just what they were doing at the time.

As the blues drifted away like a tumbleweed in the West Texas wind, I felt lucky to have seen what I saw, and to have heard what I heard. It wasn't meant for anybody outside the inner sanctum. They were real characters, larger than life, and their shows in those days were either a triumph or a tragedy, equally deep and moving either way. Townes Van Zandt's set onstage that night consisted of exactly one and a half songs before he saw something in his mind's distance that made him stand up and slowly walk offstage; that was just his Greek tragedy being played out on Music Row. The truth is, we were all lucky to have been in the presence of these flawed giants. Over the ensuing years, I would learn more and more about Texas songwriters.

Any time I could take an extra weekend off from D.C., I would hit Nashville and then continue on to Austin. I played some gigs there with Jane Gillman, who I had worked with at the House of Musical Traditions up in Takoma Park, Maryland. Jane was a good songwriter who could also tour as a utility musician on guitar or harmonica. When I first met her, she was on the road backing Lyle Lovett. Jane and I played in the front lobby of Gruene Hall, a historic dance place down south of Austin. It was a very laid-back gig, appropriate for Jane's sunny stage persona, but there was one skeptic in the audience. A particular chair was always saved for an elderly gent named Frank Slaughter. Frank never missed the music at Gruene Hall, and he was not shy about proffering his critique at the end of a show. He had the leathery look of an old cowboy, and his voice had a gritty Texas twang to match. At the end of Jane's set, the audience applauded appreciatively, and as the room quieted down, Frank loudly pronounced his verdict: "Sounds like flower child music to me!"

Back in D.C., I hooked up with Pete Ragusa, who had played drums in Bound For Glory during the Nighthawks' sabbatical. The Hawks were back on the road, and Pete asked if I could clear my schedule and do a tour with them. It was winter, the tour went to Florida, so what was not to like? As with every other adventure, the whole thing started with me saying "yes."

The band was in a transitional period. I had opened for them at one of their early shows, at the Pier Ballroom on the beach at Ocean City, Maryland, back around 1972. From the beginning, the dynamic of the band was a push-pull between two charismatic front men. Mark Wenner was the group's leader, founder, and keeper of their vision as a true American roots band. He was considered a scholar and a synthesizer of every genre from blues to country, and he knew all the common threads. His alter ego and foil in the Hawks was Jimmy Thackery. Jimmy also knew the roots, but his focus was on showmanship, and he was good at it. A Hawks gig would usually end with Jimmy walking atop the bar, playing Elmore James riffs on his Flying V, using a foaming beer bottle for a slide. Jimmy got so much attention that, inevitably, he split off on his own. That left the Hawks needing to replace not only a guitarist—they also had to find a player who could fill in the showmanship gap that Jimmy was leaving. I was not that guy, and they knew it, but they were using solid freelance players in order to keep touring while their search continued.

I got a tape of some recent live Nighthawks shows so I could woodshed the material. It turned out to be a fantastic tutorial. The two players who preceded me were Steuart Smith, one of my all-time favorites and a sometime Rosslyn Mountain Boy who later went to work for The Eagles, and Warren Haynes, later an Allman Brother, who I was hearing for the first time. They were both great, and the tape was filled with licks that I would never have come up with on my own. I was looking forward to aiming for their high standard when we hit the road.

The trip down to Florida was eventful: the power steering in the big rental van went out about ten minutes into the twelve-hour trip. The steering wheel could still be turned, if two people ganged up on it and used all their strength. Fortunately, we stayed on I-95 the whole way down, so we only had to turn every few hours for a pit stop. We made it and got a different van, which we packed like the first one. There was a stack of Fender amps and drums in the middle, with bench seats and sleeping bags arrayed around the shaky pile of gear. I did a lot of the driving because I wasn't totally comfortable sleeping with a fifty-pound Fender amp teetering over my head. The other members seemed to take it all in stride. They introduced me to the Waffle House, which in those days was the staple road food for musicians.

We barnstormed clubs down through Florida, with the southern terminus being Sloppy Joe's in Key West. The next gig was up in Tampa, a long drive, so we hit the road after the last show. I drove all night up through the Keys and then across the Everglades. I don't think I saw another vehicle the entire trip, but I was well aware that gators and panthers crouched in the cypress hammocks as we drove for hours under moonlight through the immense swamp. To keep me awake, Mark Wenner sat in the shotgun seat and explained the history and meaning of the blues. An all-night drive across the Everglades seemed like the perfect time to learn it, and I was alert the entire time. I knew how to be a protégé when a master offered a bit of mentorship. Mark explained a lot of backstory behind the classic Chess records, and he advised me to find the album "Muddy Waters, Folk Singer," with Muddy and Buddy Guy playing acoustic guitars as a duo. "That," he said, "was the essence right there."

The tour continued on, moving west through the panhandle, and eventually wound up at Tipitina's in New Orleans. Being the last show of the trip, I expected it to be epic and long, and it was. Afterwards, we packed the van and drove all night, straight through to D.C. It was time for the holidays.

I played New Year's Eve with the Nighthawks at The Bayou. It was another epic gig. Mark Wenner had a way of investing shows with importance, and I could see why BB King and Muddy Waters loved these guys. They were true believers.

The next gig I did with Pete Ragusa on drums was back at The Bayou, and it had a definite New Orleans connection.

I got a call to back up Mac Rebennack, aka Doctor John, at The Bayou. The club was the oldest nightspot in D.C., and it wore its faded glory well. Decrepit stairways led up to hidden doorways in fake piles of boulders, taking you down passageways that led out onto catwalks above the stage. It was a crumbling chronicle of garish floor shows and burlesque revues; entertainment that businessmen and conventioneers sought out back in the black-and white world of the 1950s. In the 1960s, the spacious stage was given over to rock and roll bands, who could crank up as loud as they wanted to without disturbing the neighbors: a big power station and a leather rendering plant that competed with the nearby Potomac for stench factor. It wasn't just the name of the club that made it a good spot for Dr. John, the Night Tripper. It was the dark alleyways and the black river that recalled the warehouse district of New Orleans.

As we suspected, the good doctor was rich in hipness and vibe, and he dripped with Louisiana funk like a crawfish drips étouffée at Mulate's. He came into rehearsal looking like daylight was completely foreign to him, wearing Ray-Bans, a floppy beret, a purple cape, and a button that read, "Yeah, you right." He did, in fact, say "Yeah, you right" a lot during rehearsal and the gig, which we took as an encouraging sign of approval.

He played piano while he sang, but he was an excellent guitarist as well, and when we ran over one song, I think it was the New Orleans standard, "Something You Got," he asked me if he could show me a few licks on the guitar. I immediately handed my Stratocaster over to him. Life is good when free guitar lessons keep coming your way. He played a laidback chicken scratch on an E9th at the seventh fret, and said, "You know, give it a little bit of a James Brown groove." As he handed the guitar back, he drawled, very slowly, "Whatever makes you comfortable." The words came out like a melody, and he pronounced the last word com-for-tab-la, with the accent on "tab," like the Indian drum. Even in his offhand comments, he seemed to be performing a mystic chant in swamp patois.

That night, he played in a free-form stream of consciousness, not the same songs or arrangements that we had run over during the day. It was evident that rehearsal was just to get a groove going—the gig itself was all about following the muse and hitting on some funk. He vamped at times, talking about things that inspired him, always putting himself in the context of the overall group of New Orleans players. He told the crowd that Ray Charles' fusion of Pete Johnson Boogie-Woogie and nascent rock and roll "turned things around" for all the piano players in the Crescent City. Then he proceeded to tear the house down with a smoking rendition of "Mess Around." It was hard for the band not to smoke behind Mac, because he laid down the whole groove on the keys. You could hear the drums and bass, and the horn kicks, in his fingers. All you had to do was roll with it. Whatever makes you com-for-TAB-la.

About an hour into the show, he dispensed with the hit songs, the standards, and the stage patter. A visible purplish aura seemed to generate around him, and it wasn't just creative stage lighting. He closed his eyes, dropped into a shamanic trance, and kicked off the vamp that opens "I Walk on Gilded Splinters." His studio version is one of the most harrowing records ever, and one of the most unique moments ever committed to wax. To the uninitiated, it seems to start out as a novelty, but five minutes in, your skin starts to crawl and you realize that this stuff is real. It's a zombie revival ceremony, and no matter where you hear it, you're transported to the banks of the Bayou St. John at midnight, with Marie Laveau working the gris-gris and the conqueroo.

Standing next to Dr. John, I could see the change come over him, see his eyes roll back as he started muttering in tongues. I was playing the repeated riff on the Strat, but I felt like a character in "Black Orpheus," drawn into a ritual not of my own choosing, but coming under its hypnotic power anyway. It was more than any of us bargained for, but great rock 'n' roll always is, isn't it?

The song seemed timeless, and I don't remember any applause at the end. It would have seemed ridiculous. I think he followed with "Right Place, Wrong Time," his biggest hit, and then left the stage. The crowd filed out, punch drunk with funk, and the band packed up in silence, shaking our heads and feeling the deep, dark power of the Louisiana humidity. Africa was in the house that night, and for a while there, the venerable old Bayou really lived up to its name.

Chapter 12: On the Bus With Mary Chapin

In the autumn of 1990, I attended a panel discussion at the Birchmere. The topic was "The Future of the Music Business" or something similar. When the panel was over, the participants and some friends walked down the block to R.T.'s Restaurant, which served as the unofficial backstage annex to the Birchmere.

John Simson collared me as we walked along. John was a top music attorney in town, and he and Tom Carrico were partners in managing Mary Chapin Carpenter. Her fortunes had changed drastically since the mid-1980s when she so shyly assured me that she would never make an album. She'd been shepherded by John Jennings, and his production skills on her demo tapes, combined with her great songs and unique alto voice, had gotten the interest of Columbia Records. She got signed, and she had been touring for a couple of years on her first album. Recently, she had gotten past the van stage, and now she was using a real tour bus, with a professional crew, a top national booking agent, and so forth. Her star was on the rise. Simson spoke as we walked toward the restaurant. "I need to ask you something, Pete, and you probably won't be interested because you are so busy freelancing here in town." Of course, that aroused my curiosity. He continued. "Jennings wants to take time off the road. He's got a lot of studio projects and he doesn't want to be out of town. We're looking for a guitarist to tour with Mary Chapin, but before you answer, I'm sure it won't pay what you're making now as a freelancer." I told him right away that I didn't care about the money. It sounded like a great gig, so I said yes! Another important yes moment.

Over the next few months I rehearsed a bit with Mary Chapin, sometimes just two guitars at her house, other times with her full band at a rehearsal studio. My old friends Robbie Magruder and Jon Carroll were in the group, so if we sounded like we had been playing together for ten years, we had. In January of 1991 I traveled down to Charleston, West Virginia to play Mountain Stage as an acoustic duo with Mary Chapin, and we also teamed up there for a song with Foster and Lloyd, great guys I knew from my Nashville trips.

The real touring started in the spring, around the first of March. I can honestly say that one of the most exciting moments of my life was pulling into the parking lot of Bias Studios just before midnight and seeing the big Silver Eagle tour bus idling. I loved the sound of the diesel engine, the hustle of the crew loading the luggage bays, the easy camaraderie of the musicians, old friends of mine, lolling about the front lounge. It was all filled with potential energy. I claimed a bunk, threw my duffel bag up on it, and looked around at my new home. When the door closed, we rode through the darkened streets, while the rest of the city slept, then onto the interstate. From there, we'd be traveling around America for the rest of the summer. After my years of driving back roads alone, trying to scribble lyrics in a notebook on the passenger seat, and looking for a cheap motel, I finally had a real road gig. I was filled with gratitude to Mary Chapin, John Jennings, Tom Carrico, John Simson, and the organization's office manager and general coordinator, Mary Beth Aungier, for trusting me with the job.

Mary Beth was a key player in the Mary Chapin story. She had worked her way up through the music business ranks, starting out as a waitress at the Birchmere; then she became a recording studio manager, touring road manager, and eventually a major concert booker. Even in the early days, anyone could tell after a five-minute conversation that she was a brilliant ethnomusicologist and a savvy mover and shaker. A major factor in Mary Chapin's quick rise, I could see, was the fact that there was a support team of really sharp people who also genuinely cared for her. An essentially private person, she was going straight from the cloistered surroundings of her private writing room into the whirlwind of stardom, and her team was appropriately protective. Things were happening fast.

We traveled south, playing Athens and Atlanta, Georgia, then we headed over to Nashville for a gig, crisscrossing back to South Carolina. From there, Mary Chapin, Jon Carroll, and I flew back to D.C. to play a one-night show at Ford's Theater on a bill with Tammy Wynette and Ricky Skaggs. In those days, I wore a pair of pointed, bright red suede shoes onstage. After the show, I said hello to Ricky and complimented him on his great playing. Instead of thanking me, he looked down, wide eyed, and said, in a rising tenor voice, "Man, where'd you get them *shoes*?"

We flew out to Los Angeles to play a TV show, and then continued on to San Francisco for a record company convention. Columbia was presenting Mariah Carey in her first live show, and Mary Chapin's band played a somewhat contrasting set right before Mariah.

By April, the band was really tight. We toured the Northeast, playing Boston, Northampton, and the rotating stages at the Westbury and Valley Forge Music Fairs. Then we veered south to play Mountain Stage again, this time with the full band, and headed up to the Cubby Bear in Chicago. A few days later, we played the Ranch Bowl in Omaha, Nebraska. It was there that I saw a change. We had mostly played for collegiate theatergoers, who knew Mary Chapin as a brilliant songwriter. The well-dressed audience was always appreciative, although perhaps a little reserved in their response. Omaha was different. There was a huge crowd of mainstream country fans clamoring to get into the venue, which was connected to a bowling alley, and when Mary Chapin appeared onstage, the audience basically went crazy. Overnight, she had become a country superstar. Maybe Columbia had put the promotion into high gear after our set for the label execs out in San Francisco; whatever the reason, she had hit it big.

The next night was an acoustic trio gig in Kansas City with Mary Chapin, Maura O'Connell, and Emmylou Harris. The rest of the band had the night off, but I guitar-tech'd for Mary Chapin, which mostly consisted of chatting with Emmylou's tech, Maple Byrne, about—you guessed it—guitars!

We traveled up through the Rockies to Telluride, Colorado, and played the fantastic festival there, and then wound our way all the way down to Las Cruces, New Mexico, near the border, where I bought a pair of cowboy boots. When we reached Austin, our drummer, Robbie Magruder, got word that his wife was having a baby back in D.C., so Pat McInerny, Nanci Griffith's percussionist, flew down from Nashville for the gig at the Texas Union Ballroom. That would prove to be an important happenstance later on.

After a few days rest in D.C., I traveled to Nashville with Mary Chapin to play the Nashville Now TV show, hosted that day by Vince Gill. After the telecast I went back to the hotel, and Mary Chapin went to a co-writing session with veteran Don Schlitz. A few hours later, the phone rang. It was Mary Chapin. "Come up to my room. I want you to hear this new song!" The song fell into an easy groove, and she sang it with a certain amount of sly sassiness. It was easy to like. We worked up a simple arrangement for two acoustic guitars in time to catch our ride out to Belle Meade Mansion, where we were playing a short outdoor set opening for Emmylou.

When we got to the grounds, the Columbia Records execs who were responsible for promoting Mary Chapin gathered around her. They had already heard about the song, and they wanted to hear it. We left our guitar cases on the grass and played the song on the spot. At the end, they were all beaming, and one of them said, "Congratulations, that's your first top ten song." We went up on stage and played the new song, "I Feel Lucky." I found out a couple of years later that a certain Maura Boudreau was in the audience at that Belle Meade Mansion show.

A few weeks later, after a show in Putney, Vermont, Mary Chapin and I were whisked by night down to the Hartford airport, flown to Laguardia, and then driven directly to Rockefeller Center to play the *Today* Show. Columbia wanted "I Feel Lucky" to get heard by the public right away. Once again, we did it with just the simple two guitars, although it was quickly worked up into a band number and inserted into the set.

Toward the end of the summer, we played outdoors on the dock at the South Street Seaport in New York City. We had played a month earlier to a crowd of three hundred at the Bottom Line. Now we were looking out on at least five thousand people. It was a free show, and the crowd was so big, that in order to leave, we exited the stage directly onto a police boat that took us to a mooring further uptown. This was New York City, supposedly jaded, but the audience was so large and enthusiastic that, if not for the NYPD, they would have either crushed us or pushed us into the East River! The next show was the Newport Folk Festival. On that afternoon, Mary Chapin, Nanci Griffith, Cliff Eberhardt, Richard Thompson, and Shawn Colvin all played, and I seem to recall Suzanne Vega and John Hiatt onstage as well. I definitely remember Ben and Jerry backstage, handing out free ice cream to the artists.

Mary Chapin's current chart song was "Down at the Twist and Shout," a tribute to the pop-up venue we all loved at the American Legion Hall in Bethesda, Maryland. We shot the video for the song in the Spanish Ballroom at the old Glen Echo Amusement Park outside of D.C. I loaned Mary Chapin my black Gibson J-180, and switched to bass for the lip-synched video.

We were booked to play that song with the great Cajun band BeauSoleil, who had played on the record, on the Country

Music Association Awards show. Naomi and Wynona, the Judds, were set to introduce us. We worked out the camera angles, etc., during rehearsal. There were a lot of artists on the bill, so there was plenty of time to hang around and watch others rehearse.

Backstage at the Opryland theatre, the scene was like a country Madame Tussaud's—except the characters were real. Clint Black had just married actress Lisa Hartman, and when they weren't being googly-eyed together, Clint was sharing a dressing room with cowboy legend Roy Rogers. I called that the squinty-eyed-grinning room. George Jones and Bill Monroe were relaxing in the backstage canteen. A lot of the old guard, real country singers, were on hand, and they all doted on Mary Chapin like a favorite niece.

As the summer wound down, the Mary Chapin troupe began to feel a bit of collective exhaustion. So much had been accomplished. The big gigs in New York, Los Angeles, San Francisco, Nashville, Newport, and Telluride had all been dispatched. Mary Chapin had done major national television, and most importantly, she'd written "I Feel Lucky." She was now a star, and she was on the verge of superstardom. She had a long hiatus coming up, which meant I would soon need a gig.

There was one last commitment with Mary Chapin before the touring season shut down in October. It was an acoustic duo gig. She and I flew down to Texas to play the *Austin City Limits* television show. On the plane, I sat across from an imposing looking fellow who was so tall that his cowboy boots extended into the aisle. I wondered if he was in the music business.

The show was a round robin format, with Mary Chapin, Nanci Griffith, The Indigo Girls, and Julie Gold all sitting in a semicircle. I sat at Mary Chapin's left, which turned out to be Nanci Griffith's right. Nanci had brought most of her Blue Moon Orchestra with her, but Pat McInerney had taken me aside before the show and told me that the lead guitarist had just left the band. Might I be interested in the gig? I considered that there were no more Mary Chapin shows on the calendar until her next album came out sometime the following year, and it was very likely that John Jennings would resume his position as lead guitarist. I had good music and good friends, but not much in the way of job security. I nodded thoughtfully, which Pat took as a "yes."

When sound check came, my acoustic guitar was acting up. Nanci, who I had never actually met, turned to me and said, "You can play this one." It was her #1 guitar, the original Nanci Griffith model Taylor. She was playing a newer one. That was my first instance of her extreme generosity toward fellow musicians. I decided that, when I wasn't playing on Mary Chapin's songs, I might as well play on Nanci's, since technically I was sitting next to her as well. The fact that I had never heard most of the songs, and I was on national television, didn't really faze me. It seemed as good a time as any to learn them. Nanci closed out the show with a rocking cover of The Rolling Stones' "No Expectations." As the credits rolled, I took a crazy solo with a lot of string popping, like Gatton had shown me in his garage. It was the last song, so what could they do, fire me?

This was a rare gig where I talked Danny Gatton into playing acoustic guitar all night, at the Birchmere circa 1988 with John Previti on upright bass. *Photo by Mary Beth Aungier.*

WESTERN SWING AT THE BIRCHMERE
MONDAY NIGHT, JANUARY 21, 8 to 11
FRONT PORCH SWING BAND
featuring
MIKE AULDRIDGE—Pedal Steel
DANNY GATTON—Bass
PETE KENNEDY—Guitar
MIKE STEIN—Fiddle
DAVE ELLIOTT—Drums
ARLINGTON, VA. FOR INFO. CALL 931-5058

Mike Auldridge on pedal steel instead of Dobro, and Danny Gatton on bass made this an interesting band.

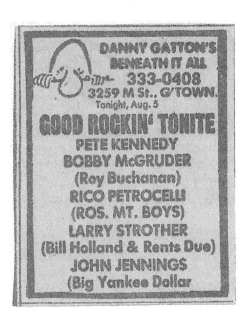

DANNY GATTON'S
BENEATH IT ALL
333-0408
3259 M St., G'TOWN.
Tonight, Aug. 5
GOOD ROCKIN' TONITE
PETE KENNEDY
BOBBY McGRUDER
(Roy Buchanan)
RICO PETROCELLI
(ROS. MT. BOYS)
LARRY STROTHER
(Bill Holland & Rents Due)
JOHN JENNINGS
(Big Yankee Dollar)

PETE &
CHARLIE'S
BLUES AND
BOOGIE BAND
Pete Kennedy and Charlie
Byrd — foot stomping blues

at the
King of France Tavern

Thursday, July 7
8:30 p.m.
$5.00 cover

MARYLAND INN
Church Circle
For Reservations call 263-2641 or 269-0990

Danny lent his name to an underground roots rock club on M Street in Georgetown, a haven for Fender pickers.

Charlie Byrd and Danny Gatton both used to call me for low-pressure, fun gigs like this one.

Mary Chapin Carpenter fell in love with the Rickenbacker 12-string jangle, and after I moved on from the band, she got one and started incorporating it into her songs.

Twangin' "Listen to the Radio" on Telecaster with Nanci Griffith on my first UK tour, November 1991 at the Cambridge Corn Exchange.

A couple of pickers sitting for a Gibson photo session at Chet Atkins' office on Music Row, 1993.

Kennedy and Boudreau; our first promo photo, taken by Pat Collins in Austin, 1993.

A couple of tuxedo'ed rock and rollers trade Fender licks — with Stephen Stills at a Bill Clinton inaugural event, Washington D.C., 1993. *Photo by Linda O'Connell.*

Listening to a playback of "Sirens" in Nashville with Steve Earle, 1995 during the "Life Is Large" cross-country sessions. *Photo by Maura Kennedy.*

Maura listens while Roger McGuinn plays his Rickenbacker
12-string solo on "Life Is Large" in Winter Park FL, 1995.

Annapolis M.D. circa 1999. This was the last time Maura and I saw
Charlie Byrd. He was like a hip jazz uncle to me. *Photo by Rebecca Byrd.*

With Jackson Browne, Beacon Theater, NYC.
Photo by Bernadette Giacomazzo.

Maura and Pete get a hug from Glen Campbell, Ann Arbor MI.

Patti Smith singing, "Strawberry Fields Forever."
Tony Shanahan on bass. *Photo by Stephen Lovekin.*

The Ark in Ann Arbor; the "Life Is Large" era. *Photo by Randy Austin-Cordona.*

Chapter 13: The Blue Moon Years

After the Austin City Limits show, there was a period of schmoozing about while the powers-that-be checked the videotape. Mary Chapin was talking with Lucinda Williams, and I was chatting with one of Lucinda's friends, Teri Joyce. Pat McInerney came over, excused himself, and said, in his British accent, "Nanci's manager would like to have a word with you." From the way he held out "w-o-o-r-d," I half expected to be called on the carpet for inserting myself into her songs. I went backstage, and there was the imposing fellow with the cowboy boots from the airplane. It was Ken Levitan. I knew about him, but didn't know what he looked like. He was a mover and shaker in Nashville, a tough New Yorker with a genuine love for the music, and he had the clout to take his artists where they deserved to be.

Levitan cut right to the chase, "Nanci wants you to join the band. Can you learn all of her songs and start in ten days?" I said, "Yes."

Mary Chapin and Lucinda had left the building, so Teri Joyce kindly offered me a ride to the hotel. Of course we stopped for a meal at the Magnolia Café. When she dropped me off, she said, "I've got a big house with a guest room downstairs. Call any time you're in Austin on your own dime and need a place to crash." I didn't know it, but that invitation set up the next big change in my life. At the moment, though, I had to focus on the present, and I needed to learn Nanci's repertoire with all due speed.

A week later, I was ensconced in my new digs in Nashville, on the top floor of the Union Station Hotel. It was a long way from the Twelve Oaks Motel across town. My room was up in the gables; with a new gig, I felt like I was on top of the world, looking down on creation. I had driven down from D.C. to get my gear there, and every day I drove over to Studio Instrument Rentals for rehearsal.

Nanci rarely came to rehearsal except to socialize a little. James Hooker led the proceedings from the keyboard. It was very different from my previous gig. Mary Chapin, understandably, was presenting herself and her songs to a new audience, and it was important that we play everything just like the record. Since I didn't play on her albums, that meant that I studiously reproduced the parts that John Jennings had done. In contrast, with the Blue Moon Orchestra, the approach was, "Hire the musicians that Nanci wants, and then let them play the way they play." I figured out which parts were essential hooks, and which parts needed to be there for the band to stay oriented, like the twangy intro to "Listen to the Radio." After those were locked down, I was free to make up fills and solos that were my own style. Nanci liked the idea of complementary voices answering hers onstage.

There were other major differences as well. Nanci was a connoisseur of interesting boutique hotels, and she refused to stay in a hotel if the entire band didn't get individual rooms in the same place. I'm sure this cost her a fortune, but she was adamant about it. She also had a caterer travel with the tour, so I actually put on a few pounds instead of the usual routine of losing weight on the road. Life was good, and the music was good. Nanci was not a country star, and she didn't consider herself a country singer. She was an adult contemporary artist, and she played theaters, mostly lovely restored vaudeville-era palaces. Her star, like Mary Chapin's, was on the rise.

The very name "Nanci Griffith" is synonymous with Texas. Not the Texas of the oilmen in their mansions on the hills and their long black limousines. Nanci's voice, sometimes dry like a tumbleweed, sometimes rich and full like the Colorado River after a spring rain, was the voice of the working people—the oil riggers down on the Gulf of Mexico and the red dirt farmers out West. She sang about their struggles, their heartaches, their sun-drenched days and their dark nights of the soul. Most of all, she sang about a small-town Texas girl's dream to see the world at the other end of the two-lane blacktop. It stretched out past the city limits, through the mesquite and the cottonwoods. There's a light beyond those woods, and Nanci grew up longing to stand in it.

With Nanci's songs resonating in my mind, I stowed the pickup truck in Nashville and handed my instrument road cases over to her crew. The cases and I would be living on a big Prevost tour bus for the foreseeable future. After two nights of shake-down cruise at the Bluebird Café, the Blue Moon Orchestra met up with the bus at Shoney's and we were off.

We swung across the Southeast to Knoxville, Atlanta, Asheville, Carrboro, the Birchmere, and up to the Beacon Theater on Broadway. I was daydreaming one morning in the lobby of the Roger Smith Hotel in midtown Manhattan, when Harlan Howard, lounging in the chair next to mine, nudged me and pointed to the front desk. "See those two over there?" Nanci and Emmylou were waiting to check in. Harlan squinted in their direction. "They're the ones nowadays who take me back to Patsy Cline and Loretta Lynn, and you know why?" He leaned closer, "Because they don't sound like anybody else." Harlan, who wrote "I Fall to Pieces" and a fistful of country classics, knew of what he spoke. Later, at the hotel bar, I sat and chatted with Nanci, and the subject turned to folk music. We talked about Ian and Sylvia, Tom Paxton, and Odetta. When Kate Wolf's name came up, it turned out that we had both been friends with Kate, and we both loved her songs. Nanci mentioned "Across the Great Divide," and she got her determined look. When Nanci got her determined look, there was no stopping her. She said, "I want my next album to be great folk songs, not my own songs, and I want 'Across the Great Divide' to be the first song. The world needs to know about Kate Wolf!" Nanci had fans around the world, and she could indeed spread Kate's songs further than Kate was able to in her lifetime. Nanci finished off with, "And Emmylou agrees with me, too!"

I filed the conversation away in the back of my mind, and turned my attention to the UK tour coming up next. For all my travel across America, I'd still never crossed a border, except for a camping trip long ago up in Ontario. Touring the UK was a dream.

We took two weeks off while our equipment was being shipped and clearing customs, and then it was off across the Atlantic. The Boeing jet wasn't crowded, and the flight was smooth. I slept, and when I woke up and looked out the darkened window, the tiny lights of Ireland were glowing way down there. Next stop: England!

We landed at Heathrow and spent a few days time-adjusting at the Royal Garden Hotel in London. I spent the days just walking the streets or marveling at the vendors' booths in Kensington Market. Everything, no matter how ancient, was new to me, and I tried every variety of chocolate bar, read every music magazine, bought mix tapes, and a cassette of The Shadows' Greatest Hits. I also bought a pair of black suede, rockabilly "creepers" and a black leather jacket. Kensington and King's Road were rock and roll heaven to me.

The first UK show was in Cambridge. The town itself—the architecture, the colleges, the river, and the shops—were all mind-bogglingly beautiful to me. We traveled all the way up to Glasgow, where a fellow in the audience bellowed, any time there was a lull, "Let's have lunch, Nanci!" in his heavy Scottish accent. We came back down through Manchester, where at the Ramada, a crowd of schoolgirls met the bus, screaming and fainting. They were expecting the New Kids on the Block, whose tour bus was due to arrive a few minutes later. From their collective groan of disappointment as we emerged, I gathered that the schoolgirls weren't avid fans of Texas folk music.

The London gig was at the Hammersmith Odeon, where The Beatles used to put on their annual Christmas shows. To stand on any UK stage where they played was a thrill; I found the "John position," and the "Paul and George position" and made sure I stood at each spot for a magic minute where they'd "trod the boards."

At the Shepherd's Bush BBC Television Centre, we played on talk shows, one hosted by Terry Wogan and another hosted by longtime Beatle associate Cilla Black. At one of the shows, the other guest was the Dalai Lama, and I found myself standing next to him on the curb outside, while we each waited for our respective rides to come around the horseshoe-shaped driveway. We did a bit of smiling and mutual bowing, and I came away feeling enlightened.

Back in the States, I was shuttling between D.C. and Nashville but I was also frequently in New York City. As all musicians did in those days, I stopped in at Manny's Music on 48th Street. The Gibson guitar company had an artist liaison office around the corner, and they would sometimes hang up a prototype guitar at Manny's to see how consumers would react. On this particular day, they had hung up a jumbo Gibson, made of gorgeous rosewood and decorated with spectacular abalone. Most importantly, it sounded fantastic; the best acoustic I'd ever played. I went around the corner and upstairs to the Gibson office and ordered one right on the spot. A month or so later it was delivered. I immediately started using it in Nashville as we rehearsed the songs on the new Nanci album in preparation for what we knew would be a long year of touring. The crew at Studio Instrument Rentals took notice of the guitar, as did Emmylou, and everyone seemed to study the detailed ornamentation carefully. It was a very visual instrument.

I got a call at my digs in Nashville. Gibson had found out that a J-2000, as it was called, had made its way to town, and they wanted some pictures of it being played. Would I be willing to do a photo session, playing a few songs over at Chet Atkins' office?

"Yes."

Chet was as nice as could be, living up to his moniker, the "country gentleman." He had his own model of Gibson tuned up, and we sat on the couch, ignoring the photographer who snapped away. Chet asked me, "What do you want to play?" I said, "Something slow." A look of relief came over his face, not because he couldn't play fast, but because for decades, he had had guitarists wanting to show him their "chops," playing faster versions of his own licks. I guessed correctly that he might be really tired of that. He grinned and said "Thank you!" This wasn't 1955, and he wasn't looking to prove himself. He did that long ago, and later in his life he just wanted to be a musician, not a showman. We played "Honeysuckle Rose" and took easy little melodic solos, no flashy stuff. I already had a note in my souvenirs from several years prior when he had heard my album "Sunburst" and complimented my playing, so I was content with that. I didn't feel like I needed to leave him in awe of my technique, and I thought back to my funny episode of "impressing" Joe Pass. When you sit down with a master, all you need to do is show them respect. We shook hands, and I left, knowing how lucky I was to sit down with the country gentleman and pick a little bit.

The next tour, over the winter of 1992, took the Blue Moon Orchestra west across the US, through Dallas, Houston, Austin, and Albuquerque and then up the coast. We hit Santa Cruz around the middle of February. We were set up for sound check at The Catalyst, when Nanci launched straight into Kate Wolf's song, "Across the Great Divide."

I played an improvised intro with total spontaneity, a different melody from the upcoming vocal line, but one that seemed to fit the changes. I was told later that the part was synchronous with the line that Nina Gerber, Kate's longtime West Coast guitarist, used to play on that intro, and I liked that notion. I like to think that Kate was hovering about, whispering those notes. I never changed that part, and it became the opening notes of the album, "Other Voices, Other Rooms" that we began working on that day in Santa Cruz.

After that extended tour, we returned to Nashville and Nanci began working on the album in earnest. One day a cassette came in the mail. It was a first draft of the album just as it came out later, but with Nanci singing and playing guitar alone. She was deeply invested in the songs, and it was up to us to provide a frame around them. We rehearsed for one day only, with Jim Rooney producing. His production approach was to simply get the right people and then let everybody play. Brilliant minimalism, and he made great records.

We were booked into Cowboy Jack's studio on Music Row. By this time, I had moved my Nashville abode from the upscale Union Square Hotel into much humbler digs at Shoney's. There, I could roll right out of bed and get on the bus, and I could always grab breakfast at the Big Boy restaurant. I was doing just that on the first day of recording for "Other Voices." There was a line for tables, and while I was waiting, James Burton walked in and got in line behind me. I turned, and said quietly, "You play guitar, right?"

He answered, "Yes. C'mon, I'll buy you breakfast." We chatted, and after breakfast he gave me a lift to the studio in his Cadillac. Much later, when Nanci's album won a Grammy and was a worldwide hit, I liked to think that James Burton was sent to Shoney's that morning to bring us good luck on the first day of recording.

We put half the album in the can in just a few days, playing all together with no overdubs, and Nanci singing with us and playing guitar. It was just like our live show, with no studio trickery. There was a guest microphone set up, and every time we sat down to play, someone else was standing there. John Prine was around a lot. He and Nanci were like siblings, cracking each other up with secret folklore. Guy Clark was there and Arlo Guthrie. The Indigo Girls came in and spread their good vibes around the room. The centerpiece of the record was, of course, "Across the

Great Divide." When Nanci, Emmylou, and Iris Dement hit the three-part harmony, it was a solemn moment, like church.

I left town for a couple of weeks, and when I returned, Nanci said, "I hope you don't mind that I had Leo Kottke and Chet Atkins come in and do lead guitar on a couple of songs."

I laughed and answered, "No, in fact I think it was really nice of you to give those rookies a shot!"

Nanci, guitarist Frank Christian, Pat McInerney, bassist Pete Gorisch, and I cut a hushed, single-take version of Bob Dylan's "Boots of Spanish Leather" one night, when all the guests had departed. Nanci was inside the lyric, becoming the character in the song. We framed it in a way that was simple and sparse, but with a dynamic energy that followed the poignant balance of hope and resignation in the words. We left space for a short solo, and a few days later Dylan himself played a two-note minimalist phrase there. Simple as it was, it seemed to recapture the loneliness that he felt when he wrote the song as a young man saying goodbye to his lover, knowing she wasn't coming back. That was all there, in Bob's little solo.

We cut the second half of the album at Windmill Lane Studio in Dublin, Ireland. One evening, I got done with my parts early, and I decided to walk back to Bloom's Hotel. As I left the studio alone, the sun had just gone down, and there was still a glow on the horizon. I heard a familiar, yet unexpected, sound drifting over the rooftops of Dublin: "Billie Jean is not my lover..." It was Michael Jackson's voice, but not coming from a boombox. I followed the sound down the narrow lanes, and as it got louder, I could see phantasmagoric stage lighting reflected in the foggy Dublin overcast. Michael's concert was outdoors, at a big soccer stadium. I couldn't get in, of course, but I stood at the loading dock, near the buses and the eighteen-wheelers, and listened to him sing, imagining his dance moves when the crowd roared. I thought back to running into him in the confines of the Kennedy Center backstage. It was an interesting contrast with the Nanci session, but, in a way, it was just another night in that most musical of cities, Dublin.

Temple Bar, the bohemian district of Dublin, was still funky in those days, like the East Village is in New York. You could buy a leather jacket for ten Irish pounds on the street; there was also a vegetarian café where the students hung out. I was sitting on the steps of the café one afternoon when a Ferrari pulled into the carpark across the cobblestone street. It would be some years before Ferraris were at all commonplace in Ireland, so I took notice. Adam Clayton, the bassist for U2, climbed out and went into a traditional music shop in an old warehouse building. A few minutes later, another sports car pulled in and Larry Mullin followed Adam's path. At that point a rattletrap (but lovely) vintage Mercedes came rolling up, and Bono and The Edge got out. The Edge disappeared into the shop, but Bono was collared on the street by a fan. I watched him talk to the stranger, and listen to him as well, for a full ten minutes before he signed an autograph and excused himself. A few minutes later, amplifiers came roaring to life in the upstairs loft above the shop. Like any band, they were practicing. I smiled when I heard them play, over and over again, a Rolling Stones' song, "Paint It Black," just like the Vipers did down in the basement, all those years ago.

I flew back to New York with Nanci to do an acoustic duo set in Central Park. The show was a tribute to Woody Guthrie, and we played "Do Re Mi." Pete Seeger was on the bill, as well as Billy Bragg, Suzanne Vega, and Michael Franti with his accompanist, the great jazz-funk guitarist Charlie Hunter. They called themselves "The Disposable Heroes of Hiphoprisy." Jesse Jackson joined us all at the end for a full cast version of "This Land is Your Land" with Pete Seeger leading the charge.

Ken Levitan's office had sent each of us an advance cassette of "Other Voices, Other Rooms" and there was already talk that Rolling Stone magazine was going to give it a rave review. Carnegie Hall and the Royal Albert Hall were already booked, as well as large theater dates all over the US and England. The album looked like a hit. We all knew that the live shows on the tour would be something really special. In the meantime, we had a few days off before the next show, a return to the Telluride Bluegrass Festival. I booked a solo gig at The Continental Club in Austin before heading up to rendezvous with the Blue Moon Orchestra in the Rockies, so I tossed my Telecaster and the Gibson J-2000 in the back of the pickup and headed for Texas.

Chapter 14: A Rainy Night in Texas

I drove my pickup truck down to Austin from Nashville, listening to my Nanci Griffith rehearsal tape on the road. Since the next show was the Telluride Festival, the plan was to play my solo gig at The Continental Club, then head across West Texas and camp my way up through New Mexico into Colorado.

When I got to town, I called Teri Joyce, and she did indeed recall offering her downstairs guest room. I had a night off, so we sat in her living room with guitars, playing old country songs. After almost every song she said, "You have to meet my friend Maura Boudreau. You two would be so great together!" I think she was working both sides of the street, because when I stopped in at The Continental the next afternoon, Maura was there. We chatted a little bit, about guitars of course, and I recall writing down the name of a certain Gibson model, "Advanced Jumbo," on a napkin.

The next night, I played my gig at the Continental. It was indeed a rainy night, torrential as a matter of fact. Flooding is a reality around Austin, and people tend to stay inside when the sky really opens up. There was a table of five or six women sitting right in front, chatting in an animated way, and that was about it for the audience. At least I was outnumbered, so I launched into the first song, an uptempo version of Chuck Berry's "You Can't Catch Me." I pulled out a handful of fast, hopefully impressive licks. The women at the front table continued chatting in their animated way as the song progressed, without a glance in my direction. It looked like it might be a long night.

At the end of the song, the silence was deafening, broken only by the continued chatter at the table. A loud voice proclaimed above the gossip, "That was *so* cool!" One of the women, the proclaimer, got up and moved to a table where she could sit by herself and focus on the music. It was Maura Boudreau. Amazingly, she didn't have a gig that night with her own band, the Delta Rays. They usually played happy hour in one location and a club gig in another location seven days a week, all around Austin and the hill country. It was a small miracle that she had that rainy night open.

The following evening, continuing her matchmaking campaign, Teri scheduled a songwriter's jam at her house. It was Austin, so everybody had good songs. I did "Run Red Lights," the tongue-in-cheek rockabilly song I'd written a few years before. I was amazed to find that Maura and several of the others knew the lyrics already, and they joined in with great gusto. There was an informal "silk road" back and forth between D.C. and Austin among roots musicians, and it seems the song had made its way down there and into the basic bar band repertoire.

When my next turn came around, I did a new song that no one could have heard. It was called "Right as Rain" and I wrote it as a straight-up tribute to Buddy Holly. I didn't know it, but one of Maura's specialties as a harmony singer was turning Buddy Holly songs into Everly Brothers songs by adding the perfect second part. She joined in without hesitation and turned "Right as Rain" into a much better song. I even sounded okay singing with her, because my rough-edged voice, the product of many Good Rockin' Tonite bar gigs, blended perfectly with her totally pure tone. I was astonished to find myself half of a vocal duo.

The next evening, I did another solo gig in the little upstairs room at Chicago House. There were enough patrons at that show that I actually got an encore. Although my set had been all roots music style, I played the Claude Debussy prelude, "The Girl with the Flaxen Hair," as a little guitar solo, without announcing what it was. Maura was once again at the gig, and she asked me, "Was that piece by Debussy?" I weighed the odds of finding more than one gorgeous woman in the world who not only harmonized Buddy Holly songs, but could also recognize Debussy preludes.

The following day, I was packing to leave for Telluride. I loaded my Telecaster, my acoustic, and my Fender amp in the pickup, under the cap and a heavy tarp. I was picking up my duffel bag prior to saying goodbye. Maura had returned to Teri's and the two of them were having coffee in the living room. As I walked by with my luggage, Maura said, "Don't go! Stay and write a song with me!"

I put my duffel bag down and said, "Okay! And then we'll get married!" We took our guitars out to a picnic table in Teri's backyard, talked a little bit about Roy Orbison and Ricky Nelson, and wrote a ballad called "Day in and Day Out" in about a half an hour. It was a darn good song, and we worked it up as an Everly Brothers-style tune.

By then I really had to go. I took off across Texas, stopping to call Maura back at Teri's number to add the words "fool's gold" to our song. I blasted past El Paso and into New Mexico. I turned north to camp overnight at White Sands National Monument, a lunar landscape that, I discovered, gets very hot in the summer, even though there aren't atomic bombs being chucked around the region any more. I continued in the morning up to Las Vegas, New Mexico (not Nevada) and camped in a rolling thunderstorm. The next night I made it over the pass to Durango, Colorado, and took the guardrail-free Million Dollar Highway up to Ouray. It was too cold at that altitude to camp, so I found a cheap motel that had a single outdoor pay phone on the other side of the narrow mountain road. I hiked across and talked to Maura for an hour or so, the first of many long nighttime calls over the next few months while I toured with Nanci. In the morning I made it the rest of the way around the mountain to Telluride, just in time for the festival.

There aren't many things in life more pleasant than standing right behind Nanci and Emmylou while they harmonize on "Across the Great Divide," hearing their voices echo off of the Alpine peaks that surround Telluride. After the show, I called Maura to figure out how we might get together again. I had driven a thousand miles from Austin. At either end of the phone line we looked at road atlases, and roughly computed the equidistant point between our two locations. It turned out to be Lubbock, Texas. Perfect! It was the home and final resting place of Buddy Holly, who we already acknowledged as the spiritual mentor of our nascent partnership.

We hatched a plan that we would each drive five hundred miles, solo, in order to meet at Buddy Holly's grave in the public cemetery in Lubbock. There was no way to make a phone call from a car back then, so we each trusted the other to actually be doing this. I came down through the Southern Rockies, beat it across New Mexico chased by a line of thunderstorms; meanwhile Maura drove across windswept West Texas. The next day we rode the "Buddy Holly Highway" (as we called it) over to Clovis, New Mexico, to get a look at Norman Petty Studios, where Buddy recorded his great sides. The studio was locked. The local newspaper was reporting that Vi Petty, who along with her husband Norm, had mentored Buddy Holly and shepherded his early recordings, had recently died, so we headed in a two-car caravan back to Austin. Maura was still gigging with the Delta Rays. I played Telecaster on a couple of their gigs: a party on 6th Street thrown by Clint Eastwood and Kevin Costner, and a show out at Willie Nelson's ranch. With gigs like that, I was surprised that Maura was anxious to move on. However, I was seeing Austin as a newcomer, whereas Maura had been in town for several years and felt that her musical options there had run their natural course. I was set to resume my touring duties with the Blue Moon Orchestra. Maura jetted off to Australia to do some busking and to take care of family business. Somehow we knew that there was much more on our mutual horizon.

In a few days, I was due back in Nashville for more "Other Voices" tour rehearsal. Before I left, I gave Maura my cassette of the as-yet-unreleased album, and a copy of the set list from the previous national tour. That would pretty much cover any songs Nanci might sing in the near future; plus Maura already knew most of Nanci's older songs. Iris Dement was the current opening act; she also joined the band to sing the third harmony part with Nanci and band member Lee Satterfield. Iris's first album was getting a lot of attention, and major labels were interested in signing her, which suggested that she might be leaving the tour to pursue her own career.

Not long after returning to Nashville, I got a package in the mail at Shoney's. It was a cassette from Maura. An expert recording engineer as well as singer and guitarist, she had done an all-night session. She'd multi-tracked all the lead and harmony vocals, with guitar parts, for "Other Voices, Other Rooms," plus a selection of Nanci's best known songs. She was one of the few people who had even heard the unreleased album as yet, and she was definitely the only person who could sing every vocal part on the entire record. I gave Maura's cassette to Nanci, and she collared me the next day at rehearsal, asking, "Who is this woman who knows all my vocal parts?" I explained as best I could, but she got a better idea when Maura visited Nashville shortly thereafter. We were having lunch at Country Life, a popular vegetarian cafeteria on Music Row, when Nanci stopped by and she and Maura hit it off. Now Nanci had a face and a high-energy personality to go with the voice.

The album came out, and the tour bus pulled out from Shoney's. Nanci was on a roll. The reviews were great, as were the sales. In most of the towns we had played previously, she shifted from theaters up to symphony halls. That wasn't just an increase in ticket sales, it was a change in the way she was presented and perceived. I got the same feeling that I had gotten with Mary Chapin part way through that tour. Nanci had broken through, and she had a hit record on her hands.

We played the symphony halls in Nashville, Atlanta, and Boston, then traveled down to the Keswick Theater in Philadelphia, where Pat McInerney took me aside for a moment before the show. "Nanci's got two days of press ahead of her in New York, and then Carnegie Hall. She could really use some rest before that hits. There will be a van waiting at the stage door as soon as we hit the last chord of tonight's show. Can you ride up with her and get her checked in to the Roger Smith? There'll be a room reserved for you as well." Getting back on the road after a show was always one of my favorite moments on tour. The bus is peaceful and quiet, our own space to occupy after the musical and social whirlwind of the show. The van was waiting at the stage door. I settled into the passenger seat. Nanci was in the back. The driver put in a cassette. The opening notes of the Byrds' "Sweetheart of the Rodeo" floated out on the night air, and even the Jersey Turnpike seemed to have a magical aura. When McGuinn and company hit the chorus of "You Ain't Goin' Nowhere," Nanci and I added some late-night harmonies. We were on our way to Carnegie Hall.

Since the venerable hall frequently features full-size symphonies, it has a very large backstage area. Nanci and the band, guests from the recording sessions, and friends and relations from around the world were milling about, noshing and chatting while Iris Dement did the opening set. There were small speakers in the ceiling, so that the performers could hear their cues to go onstage. I was standing near one of the speakers as I heard Iris start her classic song, "Our Town." As she reached the chorus, Emmylou Harris detached herself from a nearby conversation, as if a pied piper had drawn her. She floated over and stood alone, directly under the ceiling speaker, with her eyes closed. When the chorus came around again she sang a harmony, so softly that only someone a few feet away could hear it. For her, Carnegie Hall—the party, the publicists and the record people—had all disappeared in that moment. Meanwhile, Iris sang her beautiful homespun chorus on stage, not knowing that somewhere else in the building, a great harmony singer was joining her.

We traveled on to New Haven, but canceled the show because the stagehands were on strike. Nanci refused to cross the picket line, so we moved on to beautiful Mechanic's Hall in Worcester. From there we barnstormed straight across the country: Chicago, Minneapolis, Denver, then we pushed through an April snowstorm in the Rockies to get up to Salt Lake City. When we pulled up at the hotel and were waiting for room keys, Nanci pulled me aside. "Iris got a record deal, and she's going to be leaving the band at the end of the tour. Do you think Maura would want to take her place?" I was pretty sure I knew the answer, but I called Maura from backstage and told her about the offer. A plane ticket was reserved immediately!

We continued on to Seattle, and gigged our way down the coast for a solid week to Los Angeles. When we checked into the Roosevelt Hotel in Hollywood, Maura was already waiting for us.

Chapter 15: Maura Joins the Band

The Blue Moon Orchestra played *The Tonight Show*, which gave me a chance to check out one of Jay Leno's vintage cars in the back lot. The next evening was the Wiltern Theater. A high-profile court decision related to the controversial Rodney King case was expected the following morning, and the city was nervously anticipating possible civil unrest. The bus pulled out from the hotel that night, with Maura safely ensconced in a bunk. Maura would now observe and understudy for the rest of the tour. We all breathed a sigh of relief as we headed up Cajon Pass and set out across the late-night Mojave.

From the Southwest, we hopped over to Texas and played the big cities, winding up in Austin. The bus first pulled into El Azteca, a great restaurant on the east side of town, and we all piled out for enchiladas before heading to the Driskill Hotel for check-in. This was the end of the American tour, a triumphant run. Nanci was going to cap it off by performing in her hometown with a two-night live show, videotaped at the Paramount Theatre.

The backstage was a who's who of what would later be called classic "Americana" music. Tom Paxton, Guy Clark, John Prine, Jim Rooney, and Tom Russell traded gig stories and tall tales. For these shows, Maura made the transition from observing to actually performing. She sang harmonies along with Nanci in every sort of configuration: with Emmylou, Iris, Jimmie Dale Gilmore, Alison Krause, Carolyn Hester, and the larger-than-life Odetta.

When Odetta came on stage, all of us, even Nanci, stepped back. Odetta took command. She channeled the ancestors in chains, and, in the words of the old preachers, she brought that building down. When she intoned, "If I had a hammer..." we felt the power in that hammer of justice, in the bell of freedom, and in the song about love between the brothers and the sisters, all over this land. She was a true queen, and she won't be replaced in our lifetimes, but it was a blessing to have stood in her shadow.

Nanci and the Blue Moon Orchestra did a surprise gig the following night at La Zona Rosa in Austin. I was playing my fancy Gibson, and Nanci had each of us take a showcase slot during the gig. As always, she was absolutely unfailing in her generosity toward the band. After the show, she reminded us that the tour would be heading over to the UK next. She said to Maura and me "Y'all know you'll be opening shows over there, right? You'll be alternating with Frank Christian." We hadn't heard a word about that. Nanci wasn't taking into account that we had actually only finished writing one complete song, "Day In and Day Out," but we simply nodded and said, "We're really looking forward to it!" I think she knew we weren't ready yet, but we were going to become an act and move on from the Blue Moon Orchestra someday soon. In her generosity, she was putting us in front of her audience to get us started on a strong foundation.

Ten days later, we were getting over jet lag in Birmingham, England. I remember looking out the hotel window at a formation of costumed dancers in the public square. This was Maura's first day in England, and I told her "Come to the window and you'll see traditional Morris dancing, the real stuff." I threw the window open, triumphantly, and we heard the music they were dancing to: Billy Ray Cyrus's hit, "Achy Breaky Heart."

We played the lovely Town Hall in Birmingham, and headed over to Southport ("the beach" to Liverpudlians), a town where The Beatles had played frequently. That was where, on May 11th, 1993, Maura and I played our first real gig, at the Southport

Theatre. We still only had the one song, but we stretched out the set with a few songs that we had each written before we met. We knew we had a lot of writing to do!

In London, The Blue Moon Orchestra played "Later with Jools Holland" at the big Shepherd's Bush BBC soundstage. Also on the bill was Robert Plant, and Maura and I chatted with him after the show. He was totally amiable and had no rock star attitude, despite his rock god status from the Led Zeppelin era. He told us that back then he was a big fan of California folk-rock, and he thought the band might have gone in that direction, until the heavier stuff hit it big.

We opened about ten of Nanci's twenty shows on the UK tour in Manchester, Glasgow, York, Brighton, and others, and we had an extended sit-down engagement in Dublin at the Olympia Theater. Our dressing room was on the top floor, four flights up. It was sparse, with a bare light bulb, but it afforded a great view across the rooftops of Dublin. Every day, after breakfast at Bloom's, we would walk around Temple Bar, or up Grafton Street to Stephen's Green. Then we'd head over to the theater, where we would work for hours on songs, up in our rooftop garret.

On the first night that we were in Dublin, Peter Gabriel was playing at The Point, a cavernous warehouse venue. He sent a car around for Nanci, and Maura and I grabbed a ride over with her. We waited at the loading dock gate for security checks. Behind us, in the beat-up Mercedes I'd seen tooling around Temple Bar, were the four fellows from U2. They sat behind us in the venue, and I imagined them computing the production cost of the light show and other spectacular props that Gabriel utilized.

At the concert we noticed an elderly couple sitting directly in front of us. As the music rose in volume, the gentleman switched off his hearing aid and settled in for a peaceful nap. The lady, strangely, pulled out a song list at the end of each number, following the progress of the set. When the encore came, Gabriel gestured to the couple, his parents, up in our box. Mum elbowed

Dad awake, and they waved in regal fashion. Nanci went backstage, and Maura and I hiked across the city to Bloom's Hotel. The long tour would continue in earnest come morning.

Every show got tighter and more in tune, and at each show we tried to have a new song ready to perform. By the time we got to Belfast we had a full album's worth of material, but the Belfast gig never happened because of "The Troubles." The Ulster Unionist Party headquarters had been bombed, the windows of our rooms at the nearby Europa Hotel were boarded over, the neighboring Grand Opera House had severe bomb damage, and we were told to stay off the streets. Stationed on each corner was a British armored troop carrier, with soldiers who looked like college kids. We stayed inside the Europa Hotel and finished up the songs, looking forward now to the States, and our new career as a duo.

Chapter 16: Jangle Dreams and Red Guitars

When we got back to Austin, we played a few local venues, including La Zona Rosa and the Waterloo Ice House. We found, a bit to our surprise, that Delta Rays fans wished Maura would continue being a Delta Ray. We moved up to my old stomping grounds around D.C. and found that Good Rockin' Tonite fans wished I was still doing that! So—we decided to strike out anew. After having played Royal Albert Hall and other concert venues with Nanci, we weren't really aspiring to go back to local bars; we wanted to be in listening environments where our original songs would really matter. Of course, we wouldn't be playing to thousands of fans like Nanci did, but a bit of research turned up a circuit of hundred-seat venues across the US, and we decided to focus on those. We had a tremendous advantage in pitching ourselves as former members of the Blue Moon Orchestra, so we were able to quickly put together low-budget tours, tossing some sound gear and a couple of Gibson guitars in the trusty pickup truck.

We soon found out that there was a bit of discrimination to overcome from purist aficionados who dictated a strict definition of "folk music." Their definition could be summed up as "the music that was popular back when they were in college," and they rejected anything that younger people had come up with since then. Many of them were still upset about Dylan going electric thirty years earlier!

The purists didn't want to hear us (one venue rejected us as "too young and hip"), and we didn't particularly want to play for them. We started following the touring schedule of The Nields, who were a year or so ahead of us in hitting the folk circuit with a modernized definition of the form. We figured that any venue that welcomed them would be fine with us as well. They shared our view that, in today's world, there are common values among the audience that have been borne along through classic and alternative rock, as well as older folk styles. To us, it was no longer necessary to assume the role of a bearded prophet from a simpler time and place, espousing a rough-hewn Appalachian authenticity in opposition to the modern world. As effective as that might have been for an earlier generation, it wasn't our worldview, and we soon found an audience for our postmodern strain of folk.

In January of 1993, we played one of the many parties happening in D.C. around Bill Clinton's inauguration. The bash was at a big dance club. Part way through our set, Stephen Stills climbed up on stage with us. I handed him my Fender Telecaster, switched over to a Stratocaster, and we charged ahead, with him singing "Crossroads" and "Love the One You're With." In true rock star fashion, he ran his hand across the knobs of my Fender amplifier, pinning everything at full volume. The overheated amp made it through the two songs and then retired for the rest of the night!

In the morning, Maura and I elbowed our way to the front row of a huge crowd assembled on the Mall, in front of the Lincoln Memorial. The Clintons produced a series of great roots and pop music concerts that week, and this outdoor show was a highlight. Aretha Franklin sang, and Kathleen Battle did, too. Michael Jackson did the moonwalk, coming onstage after Bill Clinton spoke, because the King of Pop has top billing over a president! At one point, roadies were moving gear around the stage. Bob Dylan, who was not previously announced, strode out alone. He had a Gibson acoustic strapped on. The last time he stood on that marble slab, he was a young man singing shortly before Dr. Martin Luther King gave the "I Have a Dream" speech at the March on Washington. I'm quite sure that the import of that place and time was present in his mind. He stepped up to the microphone and sang one song, then exited the stage. The song he sang, in a perfectly clear, melodic 1963-era Dylan voice, was one he wrote back then: "Chimes of Freedom." His young cry of protest seemed transformed into an anthem of sincere patriotism, and perhaps he felt that some of the dreams of 1963 had actually come true.

As if that wasn't moving enough, the show ended with Ray Charles singing "America the Beautiful" solo at the piano, while the crowd filed across Memorial Bridge, carrying candles. It was indeed a moment, and a day, of deep love of country, imbued with a collective feeling of hope, and it was all carried by the music: American roots music.

My dad's advanced years called for a watchful eye, so we settled for a time in Northern Virginia, just outside of D.C. From there we fanned out scatter-shot all over the US. If a one-nighter came up in Kansas or Texas, we drove for two days to play it, and then drove two days back. In the D.C. suburbs, we rented basement space with room for a makeshift studio. My old friend Mike Connolly from Cherry Lane Music signed us to a publishing deal; we used the advance to buy recording gear, under the guidance of audio guru Greg Lukens. They steered us right, and we were able to do most of our first album at home. We did a few tracks at Bias Studios, and after one session we couldn't help but notice a massive plywood crate in the parking lot. My old boss, Mary Chapin Carpenter, had done some recent recording, and the studio had given her the royal treatment, outfitting the musicians' lounge with a brand new couch. We were happy to dispose of the crate, which we disassembled and then reassembled in our Fairfax basement studio. Mary Chapin got the couch and we got the crate! We covered it with scarves and colorful blankets, installed a microphone, and named our studio, "Gypsy Wagon." Thus, "River of Fallen Stars" was recorded in a packing crate.

Rather than trying to sell ourselves to our previous fans in Austin or D.C., we set our sights on New York City. The first show we played there was at The Postcrypt, a tiny underground pub on the campus of Columbia University. After that, we started playing regularly at Café Sin-é in the East Village. This was a real singer-songwriter haven. One night, we had to wait outside while record mogul Clive Davis showcased his latest discovery, Sarah McLachlan. I began sending cassettes of our songs around to independent record labels, and on a Wednesday night in the autumn of 1993, an A&R rep from Green Linnet Records came to hear us at Sin-é. He called a few days later. Yes, they were interested. The conversation continued at the Folk Alliance Conference in Boston early in 1994. We actually signed the contract at the Magnolia Grill in Austin during the South by Southwest Conference in March of that year. The rest of the year was spent hammering out the musical details of the album, including a debate among the label execs over whether it should be all acoustic or not. The progressives won out, and we were soon dubbed "folk with feedback" by a clever journalist.

Right around the time we signed the record deal, I proposed to Maura, and she accepted! We now had a wedding and a first album to plan, as well as a national tour to promote the record. We decided that the tour would be our real honeymoon. In October of 1994, we delivered the final master to the label, bought a Dodge van, and traveled up to Maura's hometown, Syracuse, for the wedding. Instead of a plastic bride and groom on the cake, we had, of course, plastic Beatles.

Chapter 17: The Kennedys

We took our time coming home from upstate, stopping off in Woodstock and, for laughs, at a resort in the Poconos. We got back to Virginia to find out that my dad had fallen ill on his return from Syracuse. The next few months were a blur of caring for him; he passed away during the winter. His last words to us had great impact. He called Maura and I over to his bedside and took each one of us by the hand. His voice was very soft, and it was an effort to talk, but he said, "Help the people. You've gotta help the people." Then he drifted off to sleep.

That moment stuck with us as, during the next few weeks, "River of Fallen Stars" was released. We took off on our first full-length cross-country tour as a duo. We'd been commissioned not only to promote a record, but also to help the people. We found a deeper purpose in making music: always trying in our songwriting and live performances to be uplifting and encouraging. I could think back ten years to simply booking gigs around D.C., trying to play well and keep working. I reflected that music, after my dad's missive, had taken on a richer depth of meaning. It wasn't just a way to keep working. It was a way to help the people. For the first time, I was obeying my dad with no objections! He summed up the overall message of his life to me in his final moments, and I understood it. We hit the road.

On the day that "River of Fallen Stars" came out, we got two life-changing phone calls. The first was from Vin Scelsa. Vin was the dean of progressive disc jockeys in New York City. His long running show, "Idiot's Delight," was the gold standard by which all free-form radio was judged. Any airplay on the show could make a career happen. We were lucky. Vin said that he was auditioning cassettes in his car; when he took ours out, his daughter had said, "Put that one back in!" They both became enamored of the album, and he did an extended special segment on it in his next show. He called to say he wanted us to be guests on the show as soon as possible.

The next call was from Allan Pepper, the owner and booker of The Bottom Line in Greenwich Village. This was a truly legendary venue, the place where Bruce Springsteen and many others had made their breakthroughs. Like Vin's show, a booking there was a major career step forward. Allan told me, "I heard you guys on Vin's show last night. I want you to play here as soon as we can find a date." Thus began a long relationship with the club, and a long friendship with Allan and his family. A true mentor, he would take us for coffee in the Village and teach us the ropes, bringing us along into the New York scene. Those two calls had enormous impact on our lives, not only musically but also in terms of us finding a community where we could settle and blend in with supportive friends when we were off the road. That place was New York City.

There was a third call that day, from David Tamulevich. David was the top folk booking agent in the US. He called to say how much he liked the album. He strongly suggested that we contact Anne Saunders, the promoter of the Falcon Ridge Festival. He advised us that it would be the cutting edge festival for the foreseeable future, and we would meet the right audience there.

We traveled up I-95 to the city, met Vin Scelsa and began a long friendship with him, then played The Bottom Line. After the show we met none other than Anne Saunders. She was indeed interested in presenting us at the Falcon Ridge Festival, and we played it five times in the next decade. It became a family reunion with our audience, and a high point of any year that we played. Our touring picked up, and our territory started to expand, covering the entire US.

We were somewhat stunned that our record, done in a packing crate in the basement, had actually assumed a national profile. This was borne out as we traveled to Nashville and then onward, to New Mexico and up and down the West Coast. Radio programmers already knew who we were. The album won in the "Best Adult Contemporary" category at the National Association of Independent Record Distributors' Awards, and suddenly, we knew for sure that we had a career.

Driving west on I-40 after a show in Albuquerque, we were fascinated by a little adobe village perched on a hill, where the highway climbs up onto the high plains and heads for the desert. We took the next exit and made our way over to Laguna Pueblo. We climbed the hill, parked the van, and looked around. The tiny town is the seat of the Laguna Native American reservation. Up near the highest point on the hill, where the old mission sits, a middle-aged woman approached us.

"You're not from here, are you?" I'm sure it was obvious. She continued, "My name is Ramona. The tribe is having a parade today, in honor of the elders. You're welcome to stay, but it's going to get hot, and you don't look like you're used to the desert. When the sun gets hot, my house is around the corner and three doors down. Just let yourselves in, cool off, and take whatever you need from the refrigerator." This was how she greeted two total strangers!

We didn't go to Ramona's house, but we stayed for the parade. That was another shock for a couple of urbanites from the East Coast. Lawn chairs were securely placed in the back of slow-moving pickup trucks. The elderly people were seated there, and driven down the main street of the town to a cheering crowd. Children held up signs reading "Thank you, Grandma!" It was not only charming, but really moving, especially after just losing my dad. We hit the road feeling that the Laguna tribe knew, indeed, how to help the people.

Chapter 18: *Life Is Large*

After three months of solid touring, motel-to-motel, with the western terminus being Café Largo in Los Angeles, we gigged our way back to the East Coast. Green Linnet was urging us to prepare another album. We booked a few nights lodging at Skyland Lodge in the Shenandoah National Park to work on songs. I wanted to write something based on *The Odyssey* that could also be a jam, using some exotic scales. It took shape as "Sirens," with Maura singing the part of the dangerous mermaids, echoing Debussy's siren calls in his "Nocturnes." We were on a pretty good roll, and we hammered out "Mystery," "One Heart, One Soul," and, perhaps thinking back to Laguna Pueblo, "Tribe." In a crazy mood, we wrote a neo-psychedelic ditty called "Blackberry Rain." We still have a funny late-night tape of us playing it for the first time until, halfway through, the guest in the next cabin started banging angrily on the wall!

Maura suggested writing a song based on a phrase our old friend Vander Lockett (who now went under the name Starz Vanderlockett) had used on a recent gig. He was telling a wild road yarn, and he punctuated it by shouting, "Life is big!" Maura thought that if we changed "big" to the more alliterative "large," we'd have a good hook for a song. She wrote the basic lyric that night, and we had another demo on our cassette.

We ran once more up the Turnpike to New York City for a Bottom Line show, and a live radio set on WFUV, the Fordham University station that was becoming a real force in the roots music scene. Program director Liz Opoka greeted us and said, "I'm going to put you with a new deejay, Rita Houston. I think you'll all get along great." We not only got along great, but became fast friends, sharing good times and bad in and out of the world of radio. After the Bottom Line gig we headed upstate to a motel in Woodstock, and reworked a few songs from my catalogue: "Velvet Glove," "St. Mark's Square," "Heart of Darkness," and "Right as Rain." We added new lyrics and arrangements, and had most of an album written. We laid down the basic tracks back at the Gypsy Wagon, and took off once again on tour.

The tour took us to the Bright Angel Lodge at the Grand Canyon. Without a doubt, it's the most spectacular setting for a gig in America, and we played for a full week, being put up in the employee cabins and eating in their dining hall. We could hike during the day, then play in the lounge at night. Most people went to bed early there, so we had a chance to try out ideas and talk about the concept for the new album. "River" had been mostly written in Ireland, and it had a sonic overlay and a Yeats-inspired lyrical flow that suggested the misty ambience of the place. The new album would represent us coming off a solid year of travel around the US, especially in the Southwest. Nothing could be more in contrast with Ireland. We decided not to replicate the sound and feel of the first album; we instead went for an organic on-the-road concept. Part of that concept would be cameo appearances by guest artists who had had an influence on us, who would resonate with our fans, and who would somehow represent the music that springs up from the American road. In our cabin at the Grand Canyon, I got on the phone.

I got in touch with Nils Lofgren, Eric Ambel, and The Dixie Hummingbirds, and they all agreed right away. We had done a workshop at the Philadelphia Folk Festival earlier that year with the Dixie Hummingbirds, and they said "If you ever want us to sing…"

The tour continued. I had put in a call to Roger McGuinn. The Byrds had always been one of our main influences. I had played the Bach piece "Jesu, Joy of Man's Desiring" as a solo on the basic track of "Life Is Large" as a tribute to Roger because he had played that melody on an early Byrds cut, "She Don't Care About Time." Maura suggested we contact McGuinn. Maybe he would reprise the Bach melody on his chiming Rickenbacker 12-string? We left a message and sent out a cassette.

There was no immediate response to our McGuinn pitch as we played our way out West and up the coast to Seattle. After a gig at The Tractor, we headed out on the long road back to Virginia. At a truckstop in Montana, we got a phone message: "Roger likes the song and yes, he'll do the solo." We ran back to the van and hightailed it two thousand miles to our studio, grabbed the master tape, then continued another thousand miles to Florida. There, Roger cut his great solo on the song. He was infinitely gracious in answering questions and telling stories about his days leading The Byrds, and about his friendship with The Beatles.

The 1995 tour continued on to Nashville and Austin. This time we brought the master tape with us. Just east of Nashville, I called our friend Ray Kennedy (no relation). Ray had a great analog studio on Music Row, with guitars hanging like Christmas lights from the ceiling. I asked Ray what he was up to, and he said, "I'm just sitting here with Steve Earle." I said, "We'll be right over!" We had run into Steve on the same day that we met the Dixie Hummingbirds in Philadelphia. At the time, he was coming off a long period of personal trouble, and some people in the business wouldn't touch him. He was relying on his renewed creative energy, and on those who still believed in him. I believed in him. I felt that opening for him at the Birchmere back in the 1980s was a great break for me. He had been generous about inviting me to travel around on his bus and hang out at rehearsal, before personal problems sidelined him, so I wasn't going to write him off.

We got to the studio and I asked Steve if he'd like to guest on our album, not as a singer but as the mandolin player on "Sirens." After the session, he offered to let us sleep in our van in his driveway out in the country, "as long as we didn't run over any puppies." We agreed, and after a night of dramatic thunderstorms, we slogged over to the house for coffee. It was 8:00 a.m., and as soon as I sat down, Steve handed me a six-string bass, the instrument featured on his first hit, "Guitar Town." Of course I played the hook to the song, and continued noodling on the guitar while Steve and his family had breakfast watching *Pulp Fiction*. I silently conjectured that they were probably the only family in America watching *Pulp Fiction* over breakfast.

That evening, we played the Bluebird Café in a loose jam session with Ray Kennedy and the wonderful Rosie Flores. Steve came, and brought along his son Justin Townes, who would later become a force in his own right on the Americana scene. I think they may have comprised the entire audience on that rainy Nashville night.

We headed for Texas to continue recording, with an unplanned stop on the Oklahoma plains. We got a tornado warning on the radio. We really didn't want to get overturned with the master tape in the van! We checked into the first motel we came to, and literally crawled under the bed. After a while, no tornado had come through. Still hiding under the bed, we started working on a song, which we finished that day as "Sunday," the last tune to make it on the album.

We continued on to Austin, where we encamped at The Woodshed, Herb Belofsky's studio on the south side of town. I made some calls. In those days, long-distance calls were more expensive than local, so it was common practice to wait until you got to a town to start lining up musicians for a project. We had met alt-rock sage Peter Holsapple at The Cactus Café in Austin earlier in the year, when we played a South by Southwest showcase. He volunteered to "sing, play, or make tea" the next time we were in the studio, so we brought him and his then wife Susan Cowsill up from New Orleans. Once in Austin, I got on the phone and invited Kelly Willis, Michael Fracasso, Jimmy

LaFave, Gurf Morlix, and Monte Warden over to the studio. It was like a constant jam session, and Charlie Sexton, on a break from Bob Dylan's band, brought over an exotic instrument called a cümbüs, putting the finishing touch on "Sirens."

Now we really had a record, and we headed back to Bias Studios to finish up the mix. We decided to name the record after the pivotal song, "Life Is Large." We knew we had something special.

It's a good feeling to have a project in the can that you are really proud of, and Green Linnet's promo team felt the same way. They went into high gear, and when "Life Is Large" came out in May of 1996, we were back on the road again. Checking messages after a Bottom Line gig in New York City, we were astonished to hear that two major publications, *USA Today* and *People* magazine, were going to give the album positive reviews. We were also booked for an interview on National Public Radio's "All Things Considered: Weekend Edition." Those were huge breaks, big steps forward for us, and they were quickly followed by another break: our first tour of England as ourselves, not backing Nanci Griffith.

The good news about England was that we were booked to play a set on MTV. The bad news was that the session was in the morning shortly after disembarking from an overnight red-eye flight from New York. Not the best time slot for making visual impact! A cab ride got us to the Columbia Hotel, near Marble Arch in Hyde Park, where our room was still being cleaned. The manager let us use the housekeeper's room to try and get MTV-ready. Making it over to the studio in Camden Town just in time, we shot the segment, then checked the video. The sound engineer had made an aesthetic decision to make us sound like we were singing from high atop the Himalayas. Perhaps he had a new reverberation effect, and he wanted to test its limits. Tired as we were, we vetoed the tape and re-shot the entire thing, sounding more like ourselves. The tour was underway.

We got settled in at the hotel, and met up with Tom Paxton, my stalwart mentor from the Nashville hotel writing session. Tom was a major star in the UK, where he was recognized as perhaps the first modern singer-songwriter, since he was performing his own songs in the Village prior to Dylan. Tom's prodigious output continued unabated, and as we traveled around England with him and his wife, Midge, in a small van, he continually passed lyrics back to us from the front seat. It was an effort to keep up with him, adding a few words here and there, but it was a great opportunity to study with one of the masters. After a few shows on the road with Tom, we split off on our own, laying groundwork for future trips to the UK and Ireland.

In London, we contacted a friend who pulled a few strings and got us in the door of the EMI Recording Studios, better known simply as "Abbey Road." We headed straight for the inner sanctum, Studio Two. It was in this gym-sized room that The Beatles recorded most of the songs on their string of ever-evolving albums back in the swinging London sixties. George Martin's control room, at the top of a steep stairway, looks down on the scene like the abode of a benevolent Yoda. We played a few notes on the original "Lady Madonna" upright piano and the Hammond organ, and stomped on the parquet floor, just for good luck.

The following day was set aside for media, which meant being ferried around town by our erstwhile publicist, Sue Williams, to meet with reporters and radio people.

At the end of our media day, Sue asked for a favor. Would we do a slot for the BBC World Service? It would involve a car ride to another part of town, and a hike up a long flight of stairs with our guitars. We were dog tired, but we agreed. The interview was short but concise. We closed it out by singing "Life Is Large" live in the studio.

Fast-forwarding a bit, we were playing a show in D.C. a couple of years later, when a woman introduced herself and thanked us. She related that she had been living in an abusive relationship in Africa, unable to find the courage to extricate herself, when one day she was tuned into the BBC World Service: the day we sang

"Life Is Large." Hearing the song motivated her to leave and start a new, positive life in D.C. Sometimes just climbing a stairway can lead to an opportunity to, in my dad's words, "help the people."

After the tour ended in Galway, we drove all night across Ireland to make an early morning flight to London, and continued on from there to Dulles Airport. We played a show the next day at Dogfish Head in Rehoboth Beach, Delaware, then drove straight to Florida for a couple of shows, after which we traveled straight back to upstate New York for the Falcon Ridge Festival. Needless to say, it was a busy summer.

That autumn, we played a radio conference at the Hilton Hotel in D.C. on a bill with Brian Setzer. The show also featured a new duo, Gillian Welch and David Rawlings. We chatted amiably with them, and wound up doing a few more gigs together.

November found us back in Nashville, at Jack's Tracks Recording Studio. Nanci Griffith was recording "Other Voices, Too," along with Emmylou Harris, Odetta, Tom Rush, Carolyn Hester, Tom Russell, and Susan Cowsill. We cut "Wasn't That a Mighty Storm?" with everyone gathered around the microphone. It was fun, after a year of intense touring, to just have an old-fashioned hootenanny.

Our Reston home studio was very busy in early 1998, with guitarists John Jennings, Steuart Smith, Al Petteway, and Amy White all coming in during the winter months to cut tracks. Nanci Griffith came in as well, to record "The Tower Song" for a Townes Van Zandt tribute album.

In February, we traveled to Memphis to play The Daisy Theater with The Campbell Brothers, and we added some additional shows at the national Folk Alliance Conference. We played a tiny showcase in a hotel room with another duo, previously unknown to us: Dave Carter and Tracy Grammer. We were floored by Dave's songwriting. The four of us agreed to do more shows together. They were looking to expand out of Portland, Oregon and play on the East Coast.

Later that spring, Maura and I made our way down to Pensacola, Florida for Springfest. We were so tired on arrival that we parked the van backstage and promptly went to sleep. We woke to someone tapping on the driver's side window. It was Steve Forbert. He suggested we do some recording with him in Alabama.

After cutting some tracks with Steve, we headed west on Highway 10 to New Orleans to meet up with Peter Holsapple and his band, The Continental Drifters. Once across the bayous, we dove into life in The Big Easy.

At the Café Du Monde, just after sundown, we drank strong coffee with chicory and beignets on the side. A street jazz band came bobbing and weaving down the sidewalk, all Gospel call-and-response trombones, with a big funky bass drum.

A crowd was dancing around the musicians; in fact there was no clear boundary between the crowd and the band, and the coffee drinkers got swept along the sidewalk in a spontaneous second line. We eventually popped out on Ursuline Street, and went searching for food.

"Y'all are hungry, right?" A tall, thin man attired in chef's livery topped with a huge Afro accosted us from a kitchen door. "Just come on in. Ain't no menu. Y'all just sit down." We did. After a while, the food started coming, in the exact same order as the Hank Williams song: jambalaya, crawfish pie, and filé gumbo. Transcendent cuisine, nothing like the ersatz versions up north. We stumbled out into the humid street. No sign in front of the place—no name, apparently. The kind of hideaway you could never find again. The kind of chef you could never track down again. He finds you.

We headed for the gig. Howlin' Wolf's was a funky rock and blues bar in the warehouse district down by the docks. We played our set and went backstage. A group of assorted longhairs and music aficionados were chatting, drinking bottles of Jax beer. Over in the corner, behind a stack of guitar and drum cases, a young man was singing in a high, clear voice. He was rehearsing a Kinks song, "Waterloo Sunset." Even though Ray Davies wrote it years earlier about London, it seemed to evoke New Orleans. It's about looking out over the river, could be the Thames or the Mississippi, and feeling the cosmic permission to lay your burden down. Everybody in the Crescent City has felt that, up on the levee. Maura moved closer to hear who was singing. It wasn't Davies, but the plaintive quality made it clear that this was someone who felt the song as if he had written it himself. Maura instinctively added the smooth, chromatic descending harmony line that graces the original version. The young man, Jackson Browne, smiled, and it seemed only right that the collaboration should continue up on stage. When they got up to sing, the raucous roots rock crowd quieted down. Everybody reflected on the river, the notion of neighborhood, and the treasure of simply hanging out with kindred spirits. It was a New Orleans moment; a spontaneous, heartfelt musical conversation. I thought back to the first time I had heard Jackson sing, as an unknown songwriter opening for Joni Mitchell in Boston a lifetime ago.

After the show, the full moon was riding high over the Jax Brewery when we climbed up onto the Jackson Square levee. In the darkness, somebody was playing the blues on a tenor sax, chanting long, drawn-out notes over the eternal moon river.

Looking out over the bayous, as they disappeared down toward the Gulf, I wondered how deep my own spirit ran, compared to the original New Orleans saints who were brought here in chains. If I were sold into slavery in this hot, humid Babylon, would I respond by giving back to the world the incredible gifts of jazz, gospel, blues? Thinking about it there on the levee, it seemed like the gift of African-American music is one of the greatest acts of charity the world has ever seen or heard: music from a river so deep and wide that we can see our own souls reflected in it.

Back on the East Coast, we were strolling through George-town one evening, and we turned down Blues Alley. There was a small loading dock with an iron door that led directly onto the stage, in the club for which the alley is named. A homeless man was sitting on the dock, with his ear pressed against the door. He motioned for us to come close. We did. He whispered, "Pharoah Sanders is onstage." He turned his attention back to the sound. As Sanders, a protégé of the late John Coltrane, intoned on the tenor sax, the homeless man began communicating with him through the iron door, in a whisper. "Yeah, yeah. Not too fast. Cool it down a little bit. That's right." To our ears, it sounded like Sanders, onstage in the loud club, was following the dynam-ics whispered to him from the alleyway. We sat for the entire set, mesmerized by the raggedy shaman.

A few weeks later, in Chicago, we were relaxing in a diner after a day strolling around Wrigleyville. An elderly lady, a Plains Indian, was sitting in the booth next to us. She accosted the wait-ress with a volley of questions. "Are you an actress? A singer? A writer?" The waitress shook her head and continued on her rounds. The lady turned to us. "Then it must have been you I was reading."

Without waiting for a reply, she continued. "When you talk to Anglos, they will tell you about deals and wars. When you talk to us, we will tell you the history of the land." She told us that she could walk around Chicago, and know where every village was. We learned to never underestimate the street shamans.

If you adopt "help the people" as your mission and you set off like a couple of idealistic noble knights, opportunities will present themselves, especially on the streets of New York. When-ever we were in New York, I would enjoy urban hiking up and down the broad, busy avenues. I paused one evening at a bench in front of one of the numerous coffee shops along Third Avenue. I was sitting there watching the city go by, when a homeless fellow approached me. I recognized him. He was a *longtimer*. That is, he purposely lived on the street, as opposed to being temporarily stranded there by circumstance, and he was a *rough sleeper*. That's the term for someone who eschews shelters and prefers to set up housekeeping on a patch of sidewalk. In this fellow's case, "housekeeping" was a flattened cardboard box that insulated him from the concrete sidewalk. On this particular day, he was carrying a large grocery bag. He addressed me, but not in the way I expected.

"Are you hungry?" That was him speaking to me, not the other way around.

I answered, "I'm supposed to be asking you that!" He chuckled.

"Somebody gave me a whole bag of hot dogs, and you can only eat so many."

I agreed, "Yeah, unless you're in that Coney Island contest!" I had just eaten, so I passed on the offer, but I was really touched that a homeless man had just offered me food.

I worked all night in the studio, and on my way home in the morning, I saw a couple of policemen prodding an inert figure on the sidewalk. It was the hot dog man. On a brutally humid morning, he was suffering from the heat and was unable to get up. They roused him enough to ask him if he wanted to go to the hospital, and he agreed. At that moment, a well-dressed woman strolling past dropped her backpack on the sidewalk, ran into the corner deli, and emerged with a large cup of water. Without hesitating, she knelt down, and directed the straw into drinking position, while a homeless comarade of the victim gently held his friend's head in place. While they hydrated him, I told the cops my hot dog story, and they nodded. "Yeah, he's a good guy. When he's passed out, we have to check and make sure he's okay." I was recalling his generosity toward me just hours earlier.

I thanked the woman and her homeless colleague for their kindness. "New Yorkers help each other out."

The homeless man turned to me and said, "Sometimes it's the ones with the least who are the most giving."

One morning we were sitting on a park bench in front of Saint Mark's Chapel, on the first real day of Spring. It was a perfect seventy degrees. A spontaneous flea market had sprung up in the little park, and a fellow was selling vinyl LPs by local artists: Allen Ginsberg, Miles Davis, Thelonious Monk. A little jazz duo was blowing some modal improvisation from a makeshift stage fashioned from an empty park bench.

On the steps in front of the church, a homeless man was inventing folk music. He sang one phrase, "please help the homeless," over and over to a simple melody of his own creation. Music couldn't be more distilled, or more deep in its feeling. He was singing for his own survival. Maura handed him a contribution, and she said softly, "Peace, brother." When he responded with the same words, she realized that he'd been singing with his eyes closed. The rich pageant around him, the vendors selling baseball caps and kettle corn, was not what drew him here to the steps of St. Mark's Chapel. He needed to survive the day, and that was what his song was about. The tone of Maura's voice prompted him to open his eyes, and he corrected himself, "Peace, sister. God bless." Peace in a tin cup, or at least a step toward his next meal.

At Union Square, 14th Street and Broadway, at the twilight hour when, in the words of e.e. cummings, "is becomes if," someone had hung a garland of flowers around the neck of the Gandhi statue. An elderly man was standing on a milk crate, singing a beautiful high tenor melody in Spanish, while passers-by, including Maura and me, broke into a spontaneous tango at his feet.

Later on, down on St. Mark's Place, a lone saxophone player was playing "Naima" on the sidewalk at Cooper Square. Coltrane's elegant melody echoed off the old Astor Place colonnade, caromed off Joe Papp's Public Theater, and pirouetted gracefully around the shiny facades of the new glass buildings. The Mud Truck, our neighborhood coffee source, was closing up shop for the day, and Paul the artist had packed his oils and brushes into his backpack, ready to find shelter somewhere for the night. I sat with him on the curb and we split a pizza from Ray's deli. He looked around, squinting, and said, "I used to live with gypsies under the roller coaster at Coney Island. People think I'm homeless, but they're wrong. My home is right here, on this planet."

In his younger days, Paul lived for a while in an artist's loft in Brooklyn. They'd sleep in the gallery, paint all day, and throw parties at night. Coltrane and Eric Dolphy used to come by with their horns. Paul looked off down the Bowery. "Sax players, man. They die young. Coltrane, Bird..." His voice trailed off.

The next morning, I saw Paul in his usual spot on the side-walk. He asked about us first.

"How you doin', man? How's Maura?"

"We're okay, how about you?"

"I got rolled, man. About five o'clock this morning. They took my oils and my canvases, but they hung around long enough to beat me up pretty bad." His left eye was closed, bruises and cuts everywhere. He didn't seem angry, just tired. Maybe he considered it part of the price of his freedom. But it hurt me to see him like that. "The worst of it, man, is that they did a number on my clothes. Every seam in my pants got ripped. I can't even stand up in public."

I walked across Third Avenue to our place, anger and compassion welling up, along with the feeling of helplessness that comes with seeing a loved one suffer. I rummaged around in my travel bag. There in the bottom, right where I stuffed them after our last trip to the West Coast, were my corduroy jeans. They were worn in in all the right places, and they had gone with me down a lot of roads, but now they would have a new gig. I took them down to the square and left them under the black cube sculpture. Next time we saw Paul, he was sheltered under the sculpture, sound asleep, wearing the jeans, trusting in his neighbors and resting like a baby on the planet he called his home.

We've sometimes been asked how we felt about not "making it big." We understood how distant the questioner, who knew us from the radio, was from our real experience, and we would jokingly answer, "Wait a minute, we're not big?" The truth is that we made it exactly as big as we aspired to be. Maura grew up playing punk rock and British folk rock, graduating to Texas bar bands; never on a path where she might monetize her talent and inspiration just to bathe in celebrity. As for me, sitting in with the National Symphony, and then driving out to a honky tonk to play rockabilly all night with Danny Gatton, was never what I considered the road to rock stardom. All of our idols were artists we'd discovered under the mainstream radar, and it was our goal to enjoy the creative freedom that they enjoyed. The aspect we never voiced to our fans was the fact that, having been around actual celebrities, their lives as corporate brands were not an ideal to which anyone serious about art would aspire, if they only saw it firsthand. Staying under that radar was a decision I made long before when I traded my Herman's Hermits albums for "The Best of Muddy Waters." Go for the real stuff, and keep your freedom. That was "making it big" to us.

⬥

"Angel Fire," our third album and the first one we recorded for Rounder Records, was released. We traveled to New York City to play the "Nightbirds" series at The Bottom Line, hosted by the great free-form disc jockey Meg Griffin. We found Meg to be a kindred spirit and a good soul with no rock star attitude, and we became steadfast friends.

We stayed on to become cast members of The Bottom Line's annual production of "The Downtown Messiah," a unique rendering of Handel's classic oratorio, featuring Greenwich Village artists performing the music in their own style, whether it be classical, folk, jazz, or avant-garde. Vin Scelsa did a moving spoken word piece, and the other cast members, including David Johansen from the New York Dolls, Terre Roche from The Roches, and Gary Lucas from Captain Beefheart's Magic Band, were all as nice and unpretentious as could be.

I had a nice chat with Vernon Reid from Living Colour about country and rockabilly guitar, and I made him a mix tape of Telecaster players. Like everyone we were meeting in the city, he seemed to be eternally inquisitive, always looking for ways to expand his artistic horizon. Rehearsals were a great hang with a new circle of creative people. We were now developing close friendships in the city, and as cast members of the Messiah, we were considered Greenwich Village artists. As we drove down the Turnpike for our New Year's Eve show at Bill Danoff's club, The Starland Café in D.C., we started talking in earnest about a move to New York.

On February 1, 1999, we left on a two-month national tour. I was booking the gigs, and I arranged for us to stay in the South and Southwest until spring. It was time to do another album, and we decided to write and record it entirely on the road, bringing the necessary gear with us in the van. Instead of booking studio time, we would set up wherever we lodged and pick up the ambience of the road on the record. We also brought a video camera, and of course, for the first few days, we recorded everything, which consisted mostly of fields and cows!

We cruised down through Athens, Georgia and on to Pensacola for a live radio show, and then back up to Atlanta for a gig at Eddie's Attic. From there it was on to Otherlands Coffee Bar in Memphis, and then straight down to Dallas for a show at Uncle Calvin's. It was a short hop from there down I-35 to Austin for a show, and then we cut back to New Orleans to hook up once again with the Continental Drifters, bunking at Peter Holsapple's cottage right through Mardi Gras. The house was a musician's crash pad for the week, and no one sought, or found, much sleep. On Mardi Gras morning, we were all determined to see the Zulu Parade, the coolest part of Mardi Gras. In order to do that, we had to be in the van and rolling down to the 9th Ward by sunrise, so of course that involved staying up all night. I was driving, and Continental Drifter/Bangle Vicki Peterson was in the passenger seat, shouting "Faster! Faster!" I was too tired to keep the pedal to the metal, but we got there, and as the parade passed, we joined the second line and danced our way through the streets. Afterwards, Maura and I drove slowly through the Uptown district, shooting video of the streets. That footage was used years later when Maura created a video for our song "Time Ain't Long." We also recorded Vicki and Susan Cowsill doing some backing vocals for our upcoming album. On Ash Wednesday, we pointed west to Roswell, New Mexico. We set up the portable studio once again in our hotel room and worked on the album, when we weren't searching for evidence of aliens.

We continued west, turning north to follow the glow of the lights on the cloud cover over Las Vegas, about a hundred miles away. There were no intervening city lights to distract us until we crossed the top of Hoover Dam and traversed the old meadows, the "vegas" in Las Vegas, into town. There we lodged and dined cheaply down on Fremont Street, the original "strip."

While in Las Vegas, we took advantage of the fact that we were celebrating our fifth wedding anniversary by renewing our vows at the Elvis Chapel on the strip. A truly surreal and wonderful experience, we judged our Elvis to be as good or better than the original, and we surprised him by singing the correct backing vocals to the classics that he interspersed throughout the ceremony. He sang and spoke only through a karaoke machine that provided the perfect rockabilly echo, and at the end, we all danced to "Viva Las Vegas."

Chapter 19: Half a Million Miles

The year 1999 was one of crazy touring, but it turned out to be just a warm-up for 2000. We decided that for that period we would stay out on the road as much as humanly possible. We kicked off the tour in early February at The Bottom Line, then rushed down to D.C. to play one song on the Wammy Awards show, where we had a chance to catch up with our old friends. Then it was on to the national Folk Alliance Conference in Cleveland, continuing down to Memphis, and back across I-40 to the Exit Inn in Nashville for Billy Block's Western Beat Showcase. We wound up that trip in Cincinnati, and circled back home to do some promo on the East Coast. In late March, we headed south to Asheville, North Carolina; Columbia, South Carolina, and a return trip to Eddie's Attic in Atlanta, then detoured up to Chicago for a one-nighter. After that we came back down to Birmingham, Alabama (I know, near Atlanta) to join up with The Nields for a co-bill tour. That wound its way down to Saint Augustine, over to Skipper's Shack, a great outdoor venue in Tampa, and then all the way up to the Cat's Cradle in Carrboro, North Carolina, after which we closed out the run at the Birchmere. But we were just getting started.

In Lexington, Kentucky, we played a festival set on a bill that included Roger McGuinn. Roger was scheduled to play right after our set. We closed with "Eight Days a Week." Maura headed to the CD booth to sign autographs, while I packed our guitars backstage. McGuinn asked, "Did you just close with a Beatles song?" Of course, he was close friends with the Fab Four.

Without further ado, he began playing and singing, "She Loves You." Since I was holding my guitar anyway, I chimed in and we did an impromptu backstage duo version, sans audience. As we hit the last G sixth chord, Roger said, "I like the way George threw in a Chuck Berry lick between the verses," then he strolled onstage for his set.

We made our debut appearance at the fantastic, jam-oriented New Bedford Festival in early July, and then hit the Massachusetts Turnpike, headed west. After a stop at The Guthrie Center in Great Barrington, and a quick hop over to the Syracuse Arts Festival, we hit the road hard for three straight months.

From Syracuse, we traced our route all the way out to Manhattan, Kansas, and from there up to Omaha, where we learned that, no matter how many songs you've written, you won't get the crowd's attention in Omaha until you play a Led Zeppelin song. Then we trekked across Colorado and up the Front Range for a show with Jorma Kaukonen in the little mountain town of Eagle. We continued over the Rockies and across the lunar landscape of eastern Utah, through Moab, Searchlight, and Parachute. After an overnight stay in Las Vegas, with a great meal at Battista's, a traditional Italian trattoria, we rolled on down into Los Angeles for an art gallery show in Pasadena, and then a gig the following night at McCabe's, the venerable acoustic club. The magic of playing at McCabe's is the rich resonance of the dozens of guitars hanging on every wall surface. They fill the air with sympathetic harmonics that magnify and illuminate the music.

We headed up the coast, finding our way to Henfling's Tavern in the tall pines south of the Bay area, then a quick duck down to San Luis Obispo, and a dogleg back up to the Plough and Stars in San Francisco proper. After a great show for a boisterous crowd, it was off to the Pacific Northwest. At a truck stop in Northern California, we grabbed a couple of budget cassettes for the road. One of them was Marvin Gaye's epic album, "What's Goin' On." As we pulled out of the parking lot and turned north, the album started playing just as Mount Shasta came into view far in the distance. It took just about the length of the record to get to the base of the mountain, where the highway starts to rise and climb over. We were transfixed by the juxtaposition of the amazing work of man-made art and the awe-inspiring work of Nature-made art: the mountain itself, a place sacred to Native Americans. We stopped halfway up and camped for the night, and from that time forward, Marvin took a place beside Buddy Holly as one of our "patron saints."

We played Eugene, Oregon, and wended our way up to Conor Byrne's Pub in Seattle. This wasn't a tour where we reached the furthest point and then circled back. Once we got out West, we were going to be there for a while. We hit Portland, Oregon for three shows on the way down the coast, including a night at the White Eagle Tavern; there we subbed for our new friends Dave Carter and Tracy Grammer. From Portland, we lit out across the state and made a diagonal turn to get back on the east side of the Rockies. We stopped in Montana at the Gibson Acoustic Guitar Plant, where the employees ogled Maura's rare EAS Deluxe, an experimental model made right there that never went into large-scale production. I had found it as a prototype at Manny's on 48th Street in New York City.

We blasted down through Wyoming and Colorado and turned west again at Colorado Springs, after a disastrous gig where they thought we would be playing all traditional Irish balladry. We hightailed it out of town and headed up into the foothills of Pike's Peak to the Thunderbird, a biker cabin on a lonely road, situated on a bed of fossils. We had fun at the gig, and the bikers liked anything we played. Next day, after checking out the fossils, we rolled back down the range and turned north to Boulder. Nanci Griffith, Emmylou, Guy Clark, and a bunch of others were playing the Rocky Mountain Folks Festival that weekend, so we headed up another mountain road to a red rock box canyon in the lovely little town of Lyons.

We were not on the bill at the festival, but we ended up playing anyway, as a "tweener" between main acts. We played a set directly before Emmylou. As the sun went down, it was time for Nanci Griffith, who had just arrived from Southeast Asia, to come on stage and headline the show. Maura and I sat in for the set, and we could feel sparks flying as she got in a bit of a push-pull with the audience. As exhausted as we were from our own tour, we could sympathize with her position, walking out on stage after flying halfway around the world.

It seems like that should have been a logical ending point, but it wasn't. We had an entire region of the West yet to cover. We wound down through Cimarron Canyon to Taos, where we took a few days of rest and recreation. We rented a little cabin behind The Kachina Lodge. Every day, we would walk down the road to Michael's Kitchen for pancakes made from blue corn and pignoli, and then, in the heat of the afternoon, we would take a dip in the swimming pool. It was a great antidote to the thousands of miles of driving, but eventually it was time to make our way down the ridge and along the cottonwoods, all the way to Socorro, down near the border of Mexico.

We bypassed Albuquerque and Santa Fe and headed straight up the Jemez Mountains, into what looked like an uninhabited pine forest wilderness. As we climbed higher, with steep ravines on both sides of the road, we began to see Quonset huts, and then larger buildings, all behind barbed wire and protected by the deep canyons. We shared the road with firefighters; there was a major conflagration threatening the secure facility, and that could have consequences. We finally climbed into Los Alamos, home of the American nuclear lab. This was where the atomic bomb was first assembled; who knew what was behind that barbed wire now? We played our gig on a truck bed parked in a little shopping mall just outside the gates.

We spent the night on that somewhat surreal mountain, sharing the town motel with firefighters from all over the Southwest. This was one spot that no one wanted overrun by a forest fire! From Los Alamos, we continued up through the Southern Rockies for the last gig of the western run, in Grand Junction, Colorado. As we passed through the Jicarilla Apache reservation, a sign at the entrance said, "Welcome to the Apache land. Out here, *Survivor* is not a television show."

We played the gig and, with a hint of autumn in the mountain air, we turned the van east on I-70 through the high Rocky Mountain passes, headed for more shows on the long road. After crossing the upper Midwest, we played Columbus, Ohio, then crossed over to upstate New York for the Chenango Arts Festival. From there, we incongruously traveled down to Asheville, North Carolina for a one-nighter, and then back up all the way to Plattsburgh, New York, only a few hours from the Chenango festival!

The gig in Plattsburgh was our jumping off point for Canada, where we joined up with literate, philosophical songwriter Richard Shindell for a leg of the tour. We played Montreal on a bill with Richard, and then drove over to the Black Sheep Inn in Wakefield, Quebec. From that lovely spot, we traveled down to Toronto for a show, and at that point the routing got a bit strange again. We had a couple of days off before the next show in Port Dover, Ontario, and it would have made sense to spend a few autumn days in the "cottage country" west of Toronto, but we were offered a gig all the way back in New York, at our beloved Bottom Line. We never said no to Allan Pepper, The Bottom Line's owner, who had helped shepherd our career along, so after our Toronto set, we jumped right into the van and drove all night through Kingston and along the north shore of Lake Ontario, coming down through upstate New York to the city, where we sang exactly one song as part of a multi-act show. We had the next night open, so we played a set at Caffè Lena in Saratoga Springs, then drove straight through all the way back to Ontario for the Port Dover gig. That is definitely in the "don't try this at home" category.

From Canada, we finally headed home where, via email, Maura completed writing a song with Nanci Griffith. The song, "Pearl's Eye View," is the story of a woman named Dickey Chapelle, who was the first female war correspondent casualty in Vietnam. They put together a great, rocking song. We traveled down to Nashville to record it with Nanci and the Blue Moon Orchestra for her upcoming album, "Clock without Hands." The sessions went great, and it was good, after months on the road, to catch up with our old friends.

November found us living up to our pledge to stay on the road, as we headed west once again to Lawrence, Kansas; Hastings, Nebraska; and Moundridge, Kansas, where we took a day's rest in Miner Seymour's prairie house in the tall grass. We wound up the tour with a bookstore gig in Wichita, then we headed back East to rejoin our mates in the cast of the Bottom Line's "Downtown Messiah." We still had a house in Virginia, but we saw it for very few days that year. For us, the 21st century had been kicked off in a busy way.

In mid-summer, we played a co-bill with Dave Carter and Tracy Grammer at Makor, a compact performing arts room near Lincoln Center. I watched their set while Maura warmed up her voice downstairs. At one point, Dave sang a song called "When I Go." When it ended, I went down to the dressing room and told Maura, "I think they've just played the best song I've ever heard." Having worked with so many great writers, this was not an insubstantial statement, and I felt it strongly. Dave's writing was beyond anything I had heard.

We played the encore together, and Dave suggested, strangely, that we do the '60s psychedelic song, "Crimson and Clover." He sang it, and when we reached the repeated chant, "crimson and clover, over and over," we kept that going while he went into a trance and started preaching like a Southern Baptist minister, but preaching mysticism rather than religion. Somehow, he threaded the southern preaching into a Buddhist-style sutra on universal compassion that led inexorably to the words "crimson and clover." The show ended with the audience cosseted in meditation, uncertain as to whether clapping was even appropriate. It was the first time they, and us, had seen a performer enter a state of grace onstage, and it was shocking in the way that genius always is.

After the gig, we were pulling out of our parking spot when there came a knock on the van window. It was Dave, and he handed us a cassette of their album, "When I Go." His writing became a polestar for us.

Chapter 20: *Chimes of Freedom*

On the 9th of September, 2001, we played a festival out on Long Island, on a bill with bluesman Toby Walker. The weather was gorgeous and we decided to spend the 10th looking in earnest for a place to live in New York City. We drove around Manhattan and Brooklyn all day; Maura stopped in at Dickie Chapelle's former residence, an apartment building in Brooklyn Heights. Before heading out through the Holland Tunnel, we stopped for a late dinner at Lemongrass, a Thai restaurant on 6th Avenue in Greenwich Village. From my window seat, I could look straight downtown through a curtain of cooling rain at the twin towers of the World Trade Center. At midnight, we got in the van and drove home to Virginia.

Resting up from the all-night drive, we slept late on September 11th. After a cup of coffee, Maura sat down at her desk and dialed Jimmy Rogers' office. Jimmy was a video producer. We had been working all year on an anthem for the New York City Transit workers. We were going to record it, synch it with a video, and also sing it live at their convention in Las Vegas. The convention was a couple of weeks away, and we checked in regularly with Jimmy. His secretary answered the phone. "Hi! Is Jimmy there? It's Maura Kennedy."

Long pause. "Jimmy's not in the office."

"Do you know when he'll be in?" Another long pause.

"He's stranded out West. There aren't any planes flying."

This time, Maura paused. "Why are there no planes flying?" The secretary's voice was trembling now.

"You haven't turned the TV on today, have you?"

There's no need to recount in detail the shock and sadness we experienced because it was global; accentuated perhaps for us because we were packing to move to New York City. We had to recover enough composure to make it up to the Eli Whitney festival in New Haven just three days later. This involved a trip up the Jersey Turnpike to reach the George Washington Bridge; there we had a clear view of lower Manhattan, enshrouded in a massive black cloud. At the hotel lobby in New Haven, we ran into Nanci and our old bandmates in the Blue Moon Orchestra. They were exhausted, getting off the bus after a tough trip across the Canadian border. Our gig started with a moment of silence for the victims and their families, and for the uncertain future that we felt as a collective concern. Each song took on an added meaning, and the first song we played after 9/11 was the song we heard Dylan sing at the Lincoln Memorial; "Chimes of Freedom."

The following week, at the Boston Folk Festival, we had the surreal experience of fitting gas masks before the show, just in case. The turnout was light, because the local media was trumpeting that Boston might be the next target, and the population should stay indoors and keep tuned to the TV. In any case, we stayed focused on the music: its power to heal and ameliorate. Maura started singing "What a Wonderful World," and when she was overcome with emotion and tearfully unable to continue, the audience softly sang the rest of the song for her. There was nothing to do, but keep on keepin' on....

Weeks after the attack, lower Manhattan was still blocked off, but residents were slowly returning. There was a need for the area to somehow start feeling like a neighborhood again. Allan Pepper, the owner of The Bottom Line, understood this, and he made an extraordinary gesture. He threw open the doors for a night, knowing that only locals would be able to get to the club. We still lived in Virginia, but we were considered downtown locals, so we made the trip up to play the show, which was dubbed, "The Gift of Music." Allan had made no announcement about who would be playing. The house lights went down, and a single spotlight hit the stage. Jackie DeShannon stood in the light, singing her hit, "What the World Needs Now." As she softly intoned, "love, sweet love," I wondered if Burt Bacharach and Hal David sensed, back when they wrote it, that it would someday be the perfect healing song, at the moment when it was most needed. I think perhaps they did.

Midway through the show, which featured an array of performers with connections to the neighborhood, Maura and I came onstage. We didn't play right away. A group of New York City firefighters came on with us, to a standing ovation that lasted for a good five minutes. As the applause finally subsided, we went right into "Life Is Large." As I looked out at the crowd, no longer fans but neighbors, my dad's last word came back to me yet again: "Help the people. You've got to help the people."

In January of 2002, less than six months after the World Trade Center attack, we moved from Virginia to lower Manhattan. Many people were leaving the city. They couldn't look downtown at the space where the Trade Center had been without experiencing post-traumatic stress, and they were fearful for their safety going forward. We understood that, but we felt drawn to this community which, through our music, we were already a part of. We couldn't have stood on the stage behind those firefighters and then written off New York.

We wanted to be there, so we took over an apartment on Astor Place, after a couple of close friends moved up into the Hudson Valley. There was a slight legal hitch in that their lease was not up yet, and the building didn't allow sublets, so we were "illegal immigrants." However, the situation helped our friends, and it helped us as well.

Neophytes that we were, we didn't imagine that the building staff would take note of two new tenants suddenly appearing. We didn't know much about living in a New York building. They tolerated us for a couple of months, perhaps due to our overly generous tipping, but when the super came into the unit in our absence and saw my drum set, that was the last straw. A notice was taped on our door, giving us forty-eight hours to vacate. After two years of planning our move to the city, we now had two days to find a new dwelling. We went to a realtor and took the first place he showed us, a classic tenement in the East Village, just across the street from the Russian Baths.

Shortly after moving into our digs on East 10th Street, we visited the Tenement Museum on the Lower East Side. The museum's mission was to show the deprivation that immigrants underwent in order to find a foothold in the New World. We went upstairs with two couples, one from England and one from Wisconsin, and they gasped as we all stepped into the apartment. They couldn't believe that anyone could live under such cramped conditions. The funny part for us was that it was the exact layout of our own apartment at the time!

On April 20, 2002, we played another double bill with Dave Carter and Tracy Grammer in New Jersey.

For the rest of the late spring and early summer we bounced up and down the East Coast, making our way out to Martinsburg, West Virginia on July 20th for a festival. The weather was extremely hot that week, so much so that the performers were sequestered in an air-conditioned house on the grounds. We were getting ready to brave the elements and head down to the stage for our set, when one of the volunteers warned us to be careful in the heat because, in her words, "You could just drop dead like that guy Dave Carter did yesterday."

Maura fainted straight down to the floor. The woman said, "I'm sorry! Was he a friend of yours?" I just said yes, and got Maura revived enough to play the set. We were in a state of shock. Dave was not only our friend, he was an authentic genius, and we all looked to him for songwriting inspiration. For him to be gone in an instant, with no warning, was too much to process all at once.

The Falcon Ridge Festival was scheduled for one week later, and Dave and Tracy were listed as headliners. Whether she mustered courage, found an inner core of peace, or simply needed the support of community, Tracy came, ready to play. It was still early for a real memorial, with audience and performers very much in shock. However, we banded together. Everyone on the bill divided up the songs Dave and Tracy would have played as a duo, and with Tracy staying on stage, each act got up and did one of Dave's songs with her. It was our next show after West Virginia, with no real time to process, but we all understood that Tracy's journey through the valley of darkness was much deeper and more complex than ours, and we gathered our resolve. We knew that we had to get past ourselves and support her, as well as supporting the audience. Falcon Ridge took on a new meaning that year, not only as a joyful gathering of the clan, but also as a family coming together in a time of tragedy.

Maura and I were the "Dave surrogates" for Tracy's entire set at the Philadelphia Folk Festival a few weeks later. The flurry of rehearsal—learning the repertoire—kept us busy, so that the stages of grief began setting in a bit later, when we got back to 10th Street in New York. The stage we experienced then was confusion; how could someone so full of life and creativity go for a jog on a hot day and simply keel over? Of course it happens, but happening to Dave, who had so much still to accomplish, seemed wrong. We were ruefully discussing this in our tenement one night in the early autumn, when our attention turned to Channel 13 on the television.

A friendly, fatherly fellow was chatting with journalist Bill Moyers. He seemed to be joining in on our conversation, addressing the very things we were discussing with stories and anecdotal bits of inspiration drawn from world mythology. He was very spiritual without being religious, and he seemed to be drawing from the same well of insight as our recently departed friend. We became instant fans of Joseph Campbell. We learned that, like so many creative thinkers, he had lived and worked in our neighborhood. We found ourselves seeking out books that he mentioned; these books that linked onward toward further inspiration.

Right away, this search, which was helping us deal with Dave's death, led to the beginning of a new crop of songs. They weren't songs that played with pop culture or roots music styles. They were deeper songs that were leading us on our own spiritual, but not religious, path. We finished up a batch of them at a lodge in Gananoque, Ontario, up on the Saint Lawrence Seaway, as autumn began sweeping across Canada.

The album needed one more song, and it brought itself to life. One night, Maura woke up around 2:00 a.m. from a sound sleep, asking me to turn on the recording gear. Since we lived in a one-room tenement, it wasn't a long trek to the "studio." She sat down with the guitar and sang a couple of verses and a chorus, then went back to bed. A few weeks later, when I was assembling the songs from Canada into a coherent project, I checked out some vagrant demos on the hard drive, and heard the song for the first time. I put it on a cassette with the other prospective songs. Next time we were traveling in the van, we listened through and Maura asked where the song had come from. It was her voice, but I had to remind her about waking up in the middle of the night to cut the demo. The chorus was built around the word "stand," and it was a quick process to finish it up with a few lines and a chanting coda. "Stand" became the title song of the album, and a signature song for us.

The album worked a basic theme of spiritual questing amid the wrenching social changes that occur, seemingly outside the realm of ethical human fellowship. If no one wants war, fundamentalist intolerance, and the breakdown of democracy and liberty, then why do these things seem to be happening anyway? These questions are large, too large to be answered in three-minute songs. But songs still serve a purpose. A song can still act as a rallying cry, or a quiet call in the dark. It might still bring a few minutes of solace, even as it raises more questions than it answers. Most of all, a song can encourage us to believe, and to act, without fear.

Maura and I hosted a national radio show on Sirius Satellite Radio from 2004 through mid 2008. We called it "The Dharma Café," and our song of the same title was the theme. The fictitious character in the song quotes jazz icon John Coltrane, asserting that she only wants to be "a force for good." We adopted that as the informal environment of the show, playing positive or inquisitive music, ignoring whether an artist was a hyped star or an unknown who handed us a CD on the street. We got national exposure for some good music, and we occasionally read from our favorite books. Our mentors, Meg Griffin and Vin Scelsa, were unfailingly supportive, and we thought of them as friends, much more than colleagues. We weren't ready to retire full-time to the seclusion of the radio studio, though. There were still plenty of ideas for upcoming live shows.

Chapter 21: *Strangelings in Paradise*

Maura had spent part of her youth in a pioneering British folk-rock-influenced Syracuse band called Sparse Frontiers. She embraced the style and sang it with deep spirit on the regional club circuit. Now, years later, we hatched an idea to create an entire repertoire for a folk-rock band that would consist of original songs and well-chosen covers as a tribute to Fairport Convention, the *ne plus ultra* of the genre.

Taking the concept a couple of steps further, I suggested that I would play only electric sitar to create a Celtic drone. More importantly, we would enlist Chris and Meredith Thompson, a pair of New England identical twins with amazing voices and a great sibling blend. With three-part harmony and our own repertoire, we could avoid being tagged as simply a Fairport tribute band.

As spring turned into summer, Maura and I moved to Northampton, Massachusetts, an artist colony nestled around Smith College. We bought a condo in the town arts center. The building was a converted grammar school, built solid in the 1930s. We started giving workshops and set up our recording gear, and as the small-town year progressed, we started making steps to put the band together. I was reading a lot of Celtic folklore, especially W. B. Yeats's book on the subject, and I was intrigued by the notion of *changelings*: babies who are kidnapped by fairies and replaced with an identical, magical substitute, so even their parents never know that their child is an enchanted being. That seemed to fit with the "twin-ness" of the Thompsons, but an online search turned up several bands already using the name. It was a quick mental jump to "The Strangelings" because that was not a real word, yet it seemed to make its own kind of mystical sense.

Everyone approved of the name, so we started rehearsing and gathering material. I suggested a couple of songs I recalled from my own younger days: "White Bird" by It's a Beautiful Day, and "Season of the Witch" by Donovan. The three women came up with fantastic arrangements that far surpassed what I had envisioned. This was a great band, and we spent the year preparing to record an album and follow it up with live gigs. Shortly after our shakedown show, Meredith Thompson announced the good news that she was expecting, and she exited the band, to be replaced by fellow folk-rockers Rebecca Hall and Ken Anderson. The Strangelings, with percussion ace Cheryl Prashker and young fiddle phenom Eric Lee, played the Falcon Ridge Festival that summer, and as we hit the first notes, an enormous full moon rose over the hills behind us. Nature had gotten into the act and magic was in the air.

In June of 2006, Maura and I crossed the country by train, picking up a rental car in San Francisco to head north, bound for Mendocino, Wavy Gravy's farm, and the Kate Wolf Festival. For me, reconnecting with the late great Kate, who was not only an insightful artist but also a good friend, was an excellent reason to travel cross-country. On the farm, we basked in what seemed like the longest sunset ever. It was almost ten o'clock, and the sky to the west, over the Pacific, was still cornflower blue. We were sitting at a picnic table in a grove of native black oak. The big redwoods are a few miles to the north, up the Eel River Canyon. A few picnic tables over to the left of us, Steve Earle was expounding on the pleasures of trout fishing; perhaps channeling resident spirit Richard Brautigan, who haunts the Russian and the Mad Rivers in these hills. A couple of tables the other way, Utah Phillips was talking about the long line passenger trains: the California Zephyr, the Empire Builder, and the one we'd be riding in a couple of days, the Southwest Chief. The sunset lingered on, setting the stage for a midsummer night's entertainment, while Arlo, Sarah Lee, Johnny Irion, and the rest of the Guthrie crew tuned up under a big oak. Up on stage, Wavy Gravy was exhorting the crowd to rock out, folk in, dance and sing and embrace their Big Mama the Earth, just as he did when he emceed Woodstock back in the day.

In May, the Dalai Lama visited Smith College, around the corner from our house. He spent the week giving lectures and spreading an uplifting Tibetan Buddhist vibe around the little college town. One sunny afternoon during the week, we were standing in a crowd on campus, outside a building from which he was expected to emerge at any moment. To honor the occasion, Maura was wearing a dress she had picked up from a designer friend in New York. It was a custom-made garment, and the fabric featured a large image of the classic Buddha. When the Dalai Lama came through the door, his eyes immediately went to the Buddha image, and he clasped his hands and bowed deeply. The crowd turned to stare at Maura, no doubt thinking, "Who is this woman that the Dalai Lama bows down to?" He continued on his way, spreading good vibes on a beautiful spring day.

In early 2008, we once again felt the tug of New York's gravitational pull. There is an energy in Greenwich Village that seems like a residual force field of creativity, an aggregate of the past work of Bob Dylan, John Lennon, Miles Davis, Jack Kerouac, Allen Ginsberg, Leonard Cohen, Joni Mitchell, and all the artists known and unknown who found their voices there. We wanted to get back, so we sold the condo in Northampton and bunked for the summer in a tenement above the tattoo parlor on St. Mark's Place. By the spring of 2009, we were moved into a tiny but perfect apartment around the corner, and we rented a recording studio space further up Third Avenue. We were back in the New York groove.

Most guitarists would rather see a photo of their hands rather than their face!

Wearing an NYPD hat, with the stars and stripes on my guitar strap. This was just after the 9/11 World Trade Center attack. *Photo by Joanne Nanna.*

In the zone...

Hands.

Why not grab those strings from above instead of below?

Maura takes flight on the Falcon Ridge stage, Hillsdale NY. *Photo by Fred Ellert.*

Kennedys in perfect harmony, Warwick Valley, NY. *Photo by M Ildiko Mester.*

Leaning in while Maura lays down a solid rhythm groove at the Falcon Ridge Folk Festival, 2018. *Photo by Stuart Berg.*

Chapter 22: Back on the Blue Moon Bus

On December 10, 2010, Maura and I were booked to open for Nanci Griffith at the Peekskill Paramount Theater in the Hudson Valley of New York. Nanci had one accompanist, a guitarist, and we asked if it might be okay for us to play and sing with her on her set. Never one to complicate matters with a lot of rehearsal, Nanci said, "Of course." She was always a believer in getting up and playing with little advance preparation, in the spirit of the Texas coffeehouse atmosphere from which she came. We played her entire set with her, and afterwards, sitting in the lounge of her tour bus, she said, "We have to keep this going!" We agreed, and I was on the phone with her manager the following morning, working out schedules.

The year 2011 dawned with a phone call from Phil Kaufman. That, in itself, would have made it an auspicious year.

I could write a book about Phil, but I won't because he's already written one. It's called *Road Mangler Deluxe*. It chronicles his storied history as the inventor of "road manager" as a job; hence his nickname, "The Road Mangler." I'll just give a quick overview of Phil's storied career by noting that he shepherded The Rolling Stones around in Hollywood, switched over to Gram Parsons and the Flying Burrito Brothers, burning Grams' body in the desert after his untimely death, and then cared for Emmylou Harris during her rise to the throne as the Queen of the Silver Dollar, as well as road-managing his all-time favorite, the great Etta James. He's the stuff of legend, and in 2011, the current stuff of his legend was overseeing Nanci Griffith's tours around the US and UK. We would be seeing a lot of Phil in the next few years.

———————————

Maura and Nanci flew over to Belfast, Northern Ireland to play the Belfast Nashville Songwriters Festival, otherwise known as BelNash. This event combined, as the name would suggest, Belfast and Nashville talent in a variety of settings around the university district. Maura returned to New York in time to do a quick load of laundry, then we headed straight south on I-95, escaping the Northeast winter. We stashed the car at Miami airport and the two of us flew down to the Virgin Islands.

We camped for a few days at the National Park on St. John, staying in a tiny lean-to with minimal creature comforts, but lots of great hiking and lolling on the beach. From there, we took the ferry over to St. Thomas, where we had a real gig. Doug Lewis, who hosted a great roots music radio show on the island, was also the curator of a performance series in a groovy courtyard arts center, with a funky but totally adequate outdoor stage. The weather is so perfect that that roofs and walls are luxuries that are frequently dispensed with. The gig also included a school show the following morning.

Even in paradise, there are classrooms and school books. At Lockhart Elementary on St. Thomas, the academic routine was interrupted by a musical program, emphasizing culture, history, and—most of all—fun, presented by The Kennedys.

At five minutes to one, we started to wonder if the traditional island siesta had taken over the school. We were standing in an empty assembly hall. Suddenly, the door burst open and the room became a whirlpool of activity. Every student was setting up chairs, and an elite corps was assigned to lug, plug in, and set the levels on the sound system. At an average age of about ten years, they were our youngest tech crew ever, and by far the most enthusiastic. After resolving a few sonic issues with the well-used system, we hit the first chords of "Life Is Large," and suddenly, we were a five-hundred piece band! The kids had an astonishing ear for harmony, singing along with our songs, which were completely new to them, in layers of three- and four-part choral style. The entire student body improvised their own hand-clapped percussion grooves and backing vocal parts, and they came up with a new and great arrangement for every song. We were interrupted only by applause and thunderous foot stomping at the end of each tune.

Some of the songs, like the normally laid-back "9th Street Billy," turned into infectious island grooves. The kids continually surprised us with their creative ideas and their ability to instantly perform as a huge ensemble, but we had a surprise for them. As the end of class period approached, we made an announcement: "For this last number, we need a few teachers to come up front and dance." The kids, of course, went wild at this notion, and they started shouting the names of their teachers, in hysterics at the very thought of their authority figures doing the twist, our stipulated dance. Well, not a single teacher took the bait. We guessed that they were holding back because the vice principal, an imposing lady who had greeted us cordially and somewhat formally when we had arrived, was watching over the proceedings with an eye toward keeping order, and who could blame her? Five hundred kids who love music so much that they can't sit down constitute a joyful riot, and she wanted to make sure no one got accidentally hurt or embarrassed. From the teachers' point of view, they didn't want to be the first, and maybe the *only* one, to get up and dance in front of the student body and the staff. So, a friendly stalemate ensued, with the children laughing and shouting encouragement at the stoic teachers, who were glancing furtively at the stern vice principal. Most of them stood their ground, weighing the odds of being fired if they *didn't* dance against the odds of being fired if they *did* dance.

After a few minutes of chaos, the vice principal strode to the stage, and said, "Hand me the microphone." She spoke sternly.

"The Kennedys are asking for teachers to help them." No one moved, or even breathed. A tree frog bleated in a palm tree outside the window, and all eyes turned, but no heads moved. We were all glued to the vice principal, who had the authority to shut down the show and send everyone back to class. After a torturous silence, she finally spoke. "If no teacher comes forward to dance, then ... I will have to do it myself!"

The room erupted in shouts and laughter. Kids were rolling on the floor, holding their sides in hysteria as we launched right into "Twist and Shout." Sure enough, the vice principal did the twist, and as she loosened up and shook some booty, she turned into another kid, just like her enthusiastic students. For a brief moment, no one was in charge, and no one needed to be. A few of the teachers, seeing their boss on the dance floor, jumped up themselves, and soon the whole room was moving in a delirious dance party. We like to think that we may have rattled the strict organization of the school day just a little bit. There's no doubt that the kids saw their principal in a whole different way, a way that they loved, because they saw that she could get lost for a moment in the music, just like them. As the youthful crew expertly packed away the PA gear, we said our goodbyes and headed back to the beach, the day's subversion accomplished.

Back on the mainland, we hooked up with Nanci, Phil Kaufman, and the Blue Moon Orchestra for a couple of nights at the Birchmere. Nanci was in good spirits, buoyed by the familiar setting and familiar people. Our motel was near my boyhood home on Oakland Street. It was a dead-end block, quite literally, with a cemetery at the end of the road, where we used to sled on snowy days when I was a kid. Now my parents were buried there, and when I visited them I could also check in with guitar great Roy Buchanan, who was buried close by. I stuck a pick in the grass by his headstone and headed over to sound check.

While we were in Virginia, I asked Nanci if she had any plans to write and record a new album. She hadn't done one in a few years, and I started gently pushing her in that direction. I proposed that we reverse her frequent modus operandi of traveling to Los Angeles, London, or Dublin to record. I would truck my recording gear down to her actual house, and set it up in a space I had noticed a while back that seemed right for recording acoustics. She never said yes, but a few days after the conversation, I got a CD in the mail of a couple of songs, with a note that said, "We'll start with these." For the next several months, Maura and I lived part time at the Best Western on Music Row, producing the album right in Nanci's home. All she had to do was walk upstairs—the vocal microphone was already set up.

In May, we did an East Coast run with Nanci, starting in Richmond, where a hotel fire kept us up, sitting on the curb, for most of the night. We continued on to Annapolis, Maryland, and then up to Bethlehem, Pennsylvania, for a show in a converted steel mill, with lights illuminating the massive blast furnace looming behind the stage. Nanci wrote a song, "Bethlehem Steel," that night.

June took us up to Wisconsin with Nanci, and after Maura and I dashed back to Massachusetts for the New Bedford Folk Festival, we rejoined Nanci for a trip up into Canada for the Calgary Folk Festival. We crisscrossed back to New York, and then down to Nashville where we caught a cross-country flight over the canyon lands to beautiful Grass Valley, California. From there, we headed back up into Canada, to Edmonton, in the foothills of the Rockies. We played a set with Nanci, then Maura and I did some sparse musical backup behind a Texas workshop that featured Nanci, Lyle Lovett, Guy Clark, Joe Ely, Jimmie Dale Gilmore, and Butch Hancock all sitting across the front of the stage. They each played songs by other Texas writers, including their friends onstage. They also told stories that brought back, for them, the good old days before they hit their separate roads, and before Austin went through its own series of changes as a city. The Canadian audience members were real roots music fans, and they knew how unique the moment was.

We boarded a little puddle-jumper plane and bounced our way back to the Midwest, where we did shows at Kent State in Ohio and the legendary Ark in Ann Arbor, Michigan. At The Ark, Nanci felt that she was among family, and she did a great show.

We left our recording gear set up on the upper floor of Nanci's house throughout the summer. Maura and I flew down to Nashville every few weeks to record a song or two. The process was very laid-back and informal. Nanci chose the cover songs, mostly written by friends of hers, but there were moments of composition that happened right in the studio. One hot afternoon, Maura, Pat McInerney, and I were up in the studio, listening to a playback. We were near the end of a solid week of recording and Nanci had just cut her vocal on a lovely ballad. We figured she was going to take a break while we tinkered with the mix, but she caught us all off guard by grabbing her guitar and stepping back up to the microphone. When Nanci's creative energy is flowing, she's a juggernaut, so Maura grabbed a Stratocaster, Pat picked up a conga drum, and I grabbed a nearby bass. It was a good thing the "record" button was within reach, because Nanci didn't hesitate. She hit a big E chord and launched right into a classic Texas rave-up that would have shaken the horn rims off Buddy Holly's nose, and when the perfect moment came for a solo, Maura flipped the switch on her Strat to the treble pickup and pounded out a snarling chord solo in classic Holly style. That was it. No need for a second take; in fact, any further refinement would have polished the edge off a rocking moment. The session ended with laughter and high-fives all around.

We finished up Nanci's album, "Intersection" in the early autumn.

In January of 2012, we traveled up to Michigan. In Ann Arbor, Nanci, Emmylou Harris, and Glen Campbell were headlining the Ann Arbor Folk Festival. Glen had been diagnosed with Alzheimer's Disease, and he was making his last tour. We backed Nanci for the first set, then Emmylou did a great set with some of her older tunes from the 1970s.

When he hit the stage, Glen's squinty Roy Rogers's eyes scanned the audience with what could only be described as love. He seemed to be genuinely grateful that they delivered him from sharecropping under the hot Arkansas sun. Even though hampered occasionally by his incipient illness, he pushed himself vocally, going for those poignant high notes. He also played chorus after chorus of extended, inventive guitar solos.

Glen bid the audience good night, assuring them that "a better place awaits," and the evening ended with Maura and Emmylou harmonizing on a duet verse of "Don't That Road Look Rough and Rocky." I know we were all thinking of Glen and his road.

Afterwards, I compared him to Django Reinhardt, and his face lit up even more: "Do you have his stuff? He's the best I ever heard!"

As we posed for a picture, Maura gave him a peck on the cheek and said, "I love you!" and maybe that really is what it's all about; say it to someone, while they can hear you clearly, while the Wichita Lineman is still on the line.

In late February 2012, Maura and I boarded an Aer Lingus red-eye flight over to Dublin, meeting up over an airport breakfast with Nanci's driver Oliver Mckerr, who ferried us up to Madison's Hotel in Belfast. Nanci and Phil arrived later in the day from London. We were booked once again at the songwriting festival, but Nanci enlisted us in an important side trip while we were in town. Earlier, Maura and I had taken a cab ride up the Falls Road, in the Catholic district, and then through the heavily fortified gate of the Berlin-style wall that separated the neighborhood from the Protestants who lived on the Shankill Road just a few yards away. We were aware that old cultural resentments still simmered beneath the surface.

The music scene and economic prosperity, especially surrounding the docks area, where *Game of Thrones* had its production facilities, had brought a longing for peace to the younger generation. We were glad to play a small role in the musical *rapprochement*. In the gym of a Protestant elementary school, we gathered with the students and their special guests: a busload of Catholic school children. The two schools sat in alternating rows, so that quite often, they harmonized together. Facing them, we could see the whole group turn into a gaggle of kids—not representatives of political or religious factions—just kids. The day started with all of them singing a traditional Irish children's song, one sung on every street, Catholic and Protestant. They all raised their voices together, laughing and singing, "I'll Tell Me Ma."

Next, we entertained them with songs, stories, and some discussion prompted by their smart questions. When we asked how many had ever written a song, almost every hand went up! When Nanci sang "It's a Hard Life Wherever You Go," the kids listened attentively, pondering her commentary on the life that they lived on either side of the concrete wall that divided their neighborhoods after sundown.

Then it was time for the kids to entertain and enlighten us. A young guitarist showed his stuff, playing a classic rock riff. Interestingly, he skipped over a string at the same point every time, creating a jarring angularity that we all actually got to like after a few repetitions. When I tried to join in, he abruptly played a final chord and sat down, headed no doubt for a solo career of unexpected syncopations. He was followed by a small boy who wielded a trombone which, with slide extended, exceeded his own length by about a foot. He launched into a spirited solo piece, aiming the horn triumphantly upward and captivating us all with his enthusiasm and perfect intonation.

After that, there was an ensemble dance routine that we thought might be traditional step dancing, but turned out to be skillful hip-hop choreography. Then came the *pièce de résistance*. A young girl announced that she would read a letter she composed, in the character of an Irish immigrant to New York, describing the hardship of the passage and the emigrant's combination of homesickness and hope for a better life in the New World. As she read, she transcended her own childhood and became a great Irish writer. The room was silent at the end, with the Americans and Irish lost in the poignancy of her story and the artistry of her composition. Then we all erupted into applause, and it was time for a group photo: all one group, not Catholic or Protestant, American, Irish, or British, just a roomful of kids and itinerant musicians who spent the morning sharing the things they all loved.

As the songwriting festival drew to a close, Oliver packed the band and gear in his van and drove us to the South. I watched the road, mentally teaching myself how to drive on the left. Crossing the border into the Republic of Ireland happened with no fanfare at all. This was in stark contrast to our tours in the early 1990s, when the tour bus would slowly navigate a concrete maze, and British soldiers with dogs and machine guns would come on board the bus to check papers. That was all gone by 2012. We met up with drummer Pat McInerney and stage manager Bruce Mackay in Drogheda (rhymes with "Prada.") It was at the hotel pub there that Oliver suggested that we make the tour (which took us all the way around Ireland) even more interesting by sampling the fish stew in every town. We all agreed that it was a good plan, and we started right then with an excellent bowl of chowder. Then it was on to Navan, Ennis, Galway, Kilkenny, Cork, Wexford, Waterford, and finally Dublin. The consensus was that the Old Ground Hotel in the very traditional city of Ennis did, in fact, have the best fish chowder in all of Ireland.

From Dublin, we hopped over to Glasgow for an interview on the Ricky Ross BBC Radio program and a performance at the Royal Concert Hall. Then it was down to Manchester and Birmingham, followed by a few days' stopover in London. I took the train from London over to Bristol one morning, and as the train passed through the beautiful sandstone Georgian town of Bath, I made a mental note to return there at the first opportunity. The entire town looked like an integrated work of art, and it captured my imagination in the few moments that the train was stopped at the platform.

We crisscrossed England for the next few weeks, then, after the last gig, Maura and I jumped on a plane in Manchester and headed over to Paris for a little rest and relaxation. Maura had booked us into the Hotel de France Quartier Latin, and the name says it all. From our digs on the upper floor of the tiny hotel, we could venture all over the Left Bank, grabbing a quick sweet or savory crepe if we got hungry. We played a show, on a double bill with Hannah Judson, at OPA, a groovy Parisian basement club, appropriately late-night and dimly lit. During the days, we strolled the outdoor markets and the book stalls along the Seine, and Maura took a croissant baking class; I was the beneficiary of the baked goods afterwards as we sat on the bank of the Ile de France in the springtime sun. Erstwhile road manager Phil Kaufman and our stateside friend Vicki Bailey popped over to Paris. We all spent a few days cruising the Seine, savoring the ice cream at the outdoor carts in front of the Louvre, and listening to jazz in the cafés up on Montmartre. A great way to relax after a long tour!

The next trip was out to Denver for a show with Greg Brown, then we were off to England once more. This time, I contacted a booking agency that specialized in booking American roots acts for tours in England. They had a circuit of smaller venues in place. I had a sense that Nanci wanted to cut back on touring after thirty straight years, so if Maura and I wanted to keep playing the UK, it would likely be on our own.

The booking agents, Bob Butler and Claire Stein, came to Nanci's show in Bristol at Colston Hall, a venerable venue that had hosted The Beatles and Buddy Holly. We hit it off with them, and in fact we became great friends, not only doing business but also sharing meals, hikes, and insightful conversation in subsequent years.

With Nanci, we played an old rock palace, the Shepherd's Bush Empire. We followed that with a show under the grandstands of the Chelsea Football Club, in a large pub called the Irish Village. From there we traveled up to the Cambridge Folk Festival, where we played for a huge crowd, a set that was televised later on the BBC.

The last gig of the tour was in Edinburgh, Scotland, and the band and gear trundled onto British Rail for a great ride up the East Coast, along the North Sea and into the lovely old city. Maura and I had lunch at the tea shop in Edinburgh Castle, and the gig was in the beautiful Queen's Hall. Like other historic UK cities, including York, Cambridge, and Shrewsbury, it was a great town to practice the art of strolling.

Chapter 23: *On Our Own in England*

A few months later, in October of 2012, we flew back to London to play our own duo show at The Half Moon in Putney, just south of the Thames. Putney is centrally located between Surrey, Richmond, and Shepherd's Bush, and it was a nerve center for British rock in the heyday. Three guitarists, Clapton, Beck, and Page, grew up in the nearby area. The Half Moon was a launching pad for Fairport Convention, The Yardbirds, The Who, The Kinks, Kate Bush, U2, and on and on. The Rolling Stones not only played early shows there; even in more recent times they booked the back room for private gigs. Edward Rogers, one-half of our best-friends-in-the-building Edward and Melani, flew over from New York to open the show, and I played guitar for him. Edward and Melani were close friends with Zombies lead singer Colin Blunstone, and Colin was kind enough to come out to the show, saying afterwards that it reminded him of why he got into music.

We were staying in Esher, Surrey, a bucolic Tudor-style village outside of London where George Harrison made his digs back in the Beatles era. As a matter of fact, the place was a few yards from the gates to the private estate where Harrison had lived in a groovy outbuilding. The night before the Half Moon show, we spent a fairly wild evening at The Chelsea Arts Club, a private lodge whose members included all types of artists and general eccentrics. The merriment was tempered with the news that a genuinely perfect storm, dubbed Hurricane Sandy, was heading straight for New York.

From Esher, all we could do was watch the BBC and follow the hurricane's steady march toward our home. When it hit, the airports shut down and we started retooling our trip home. Then came the news that the East Village was largely underwater. Whether that included our block or not was a question mark, and our car was parked in an underground lot.

We flew back on the first day that JFK International Airport reopened, and we were advised at Heathrow to call ahead and book a private car to take us into Manhattan. There was no gasoline available, and there would be no taxicabs. We flew into a darkened metro area; it was surreal to look across the East River at a Manhattan skyline with no lights on. Miraculously, our hired car did in fact show up, and we climbed fifteen flights of stairs to our apartment with only a flashlight to guide us. We grabbed a few things, hiked back down, found our car, undamaged and thankfully with half a tank of gas. Then we headed out of the darkened city to meet up with Nanci Griffith, down on the Eastern Shore of Maryland, to begin another tour.

In January of 2013 we ventured upstate to play an all-Buddy Holly-songs show, and then we hopped on a plane once again across the Atlantic to play Belfast with Nanci. From there, we flew to Scandinavia, over the snowbound Scottish Highlands, to Oslo, Norway, for a gig at the National Concert Hall.

Back in New York, we did laundry and climbed on the tour bus for shows with Nanci in Chicago and finally at The Ark in Ann Arbor, Michigan. I'd always felt that Nanci considered that venue her home, and the family that ran the venerable place to be a nurturing family to her. She did a great show, and afterwards, I was walking past her dressing room when she called to me. "Pete!" I poked my head in the door, and she shouted, "That was fantastic!" Nanci was usually road-weary and ready to relax after ninety minutes of giving her all, and she was not typically given to glowing exclamations about the show just past, so I took note of the unusual moment and congratulated her right back.

Maura and I flew from Detroit down to North Carolina to play some shows and get the jump on spring, returning to New York City in time for the annual WFUV Gala. These were private parties for a few hundred supporters of the station, and the "party bands," over the years that we attended, included Levon Helm's group, Los Lobos, Chris Isaak, Mavis Staples, and Rosanne Cash. Needless to say, it was truly a gala with great music. Maura would usually get a New Orleans-style second line parade going, or, in the case of the Los Lobos show, she'd organize a cadre of go-go dancers to jump on stage, much to the delight of the band.

For a number of years Maura and I played the grassroots non-profit Theater Within's annual John Lennon Tribute shows on Broadway. We typically did a couple of tunes on our own, then made the stage our local habitation, jamming in a casual way with pop mavens Marshall Crenshaw, Cyndi Lauper, Willie Nile and Syd Straw, New York Doll David Johansen, bassist Tony Garnier, poet Patti Smith, bluesman Taj Mahal, and Blondie icon Debbie Harry, among numerous other Lennon devotees. One memorable show ended with the entire cast joining soul great Ben E. King for a heartfelt version of his hit, "Stand by Me."

Sometimes, especially in Europe, we are presented as "Americana" artists and we are proud of that. We do follow in hallowed, daunting footsteps, but if Muddy, Buddy, Nanci, and Townes simply sang the truth as they knew it, then we honor them best by doing the same. That was our mission as we once again boarded a Boeing 757 bound for Europe.

In the west of Ireland, we drove the narrow back roads and stopped at an ancient monastery ruin. It was a hot day and the surrounding village seemed empty, so we strolled alone through the old stone structures surrounding an overgrown courtyard. In a fallen-down gallery, we were surprised to hear voices. An elderly woman and a young man had joined us. She pointed across the stream adjacent to the grounds, at a small cottage, and spoke in a cracked brogue. "I grew up there, long ago. I know this place.

The monks buried their dead in the courtyard for five hundred years, with no grave markings, but I know where each one is. We're walking over them now." We took a photo of the pair. When we went through our pictures later in the day, we found the photo of the young man, but inexplicably, he was standing next to an equally young woman, who looked like our raconteur might have seventy years prior to our conversation. With no explanation except that we were in the ghost-inhabited west of Ireland, we continued on.

We spent an invigorating evening at the John B. Keane pub in Listowel, where the bartender rang a brass bell whenever a patron wanted to sing. The singer would simply stand up at their table, or turn around on their barstool to address the crowded room. The songs alternated between Leonard Cohen and Tom Waits classics and traditional Irish songs of deep cultural import. It was an inspiring night of music and camaraderie. After completing our Irish circuit of gigs, we drove all night from Limerick to Dublin and boarded an early morning ferry across the choppy Irish Sea to England.

We arrived early to the Caroline Social Club in Saltaire, England. We parked the car and strolled down an intriguing alleyway decked with vines. Honeybees buzzed about, continuing the industrial tradition of the site. We found ourselves in a derelict section of the old mill that had been converted into "allotments;" what we in the States would call community gardens. These were common in our hometown, the East Village in Manhattan, so we strolled in, curious and seemingly alone.

Suddenly a voice hailed us from behind a dense grapevine, and into the sunlight stepped a character straight out of Dickens. She greeted us gaily, as if we belonged there, and beckoned for us to follow behind the grape arbor to her allotment. There she had an astonishing array of fruits and vegetables growing among the bricks and concrete slabs of the old mill. I took note of the fact that most of her crop was related to making jam, a staple of afternoon tea, served with scones. She had a little greenhouse with everything from nascent cornstalks to chili peppers, but she saved the best for last. She pointed behind a makeshift wooden fence. "Do you want to visit the bees?" I had never voluntarily visited bees, but we poked our heads in and gave a quick wave. "They're very well-behaved," assured Betty, our hostess. "The college students who come in once a week won't go near them. They don't even want to get their hands dirty!" She was an old-school gardener, an approach that was quite literally bearing fruit. And she was a bee-talker. She said the hives around the world are suffering from climate change and habitat erosion, but the solution, she asserted, lay in a closer friendship between humans and their pollinating allies. She gave an example. "I gave two hives to my son-in-law. After two weeks, he called and said they weren't producing, and I said, 'Well, did you talk to them?'" She shook her head incredulously. "How do you expect bees to produce if you don't talk to them?"

Chapter 24: A Million Miles

We returned to New York, relaxed for the month of July, then in August we played a bill with pop icon Matthew Sweet at the City Winery. We continued resting up, looking forward to yet another busy tour in September.

We flew out to Los Angeles and played a show with Buffy Ford Stewart at McCabe's. The gig was a tribute to her late husband, and our dear friend, John Stewart. From Los Angeles we moved on down to San Diego, with a few days off in Laguna Beach, then we headed out for shows in Albuquerque and Phoenix. We drove Route 66 across the Mojave Desert through Arizona into New Mexico. It took us through Needles, Two Guns, Twin Arrows, and the Jackrabbit Stop before the long slow climb up to the cool pine forest of the Coconino, where we spent the night in Flagstaff. The road had been upgraded to Interstate 40, but the terrain was still the same, and it won't change for another billion years or so. Our view out the window was the same one that Tom Joad saw in *The Grapes of Wrath*. We shared his sense of awe mixed with dread as we crossed a land meant for horned toads and roadrunners, not humans.

Provisions packed, we headed out into the desert. The terrain (shades of purples and pinks depending on the angle of the sun) was forbidding, yet lovely. The scenery was unchanging for four hours, so we scanned the AM radio, hoping to find a soundtrack that fit those craggy mountains and dry washes.

The first song that came on was vintage Ricky Nelson, "A Little Too Much." James Burton's Telecaster crackled and snarled, a musical sidewinder. We knew we'd hit pay dirt as we passed the exit for the road north to Bakersfield and Buck Owens came on the radio, harmonizing with Don Rich in a high, lonesome sound that blended with the Mojave like a native flute. Next up was Tammy Wynette, "Your Good Girl's Gonna Go Bad." That's the real stuff, the stuff that holds up out there. Right after Tammy came the ominous echoing boom-chucks of a Sun record. It was Johnny Cash, and he'd fallen into a burning ring of fire; a man singing from Hell. If there was ever perfect desert music, that was it.

Later in the day, as we crossed into Arizona, the terrain turned fire red as the sunset hit the already burnt-red clay in fantastic formations. It was there that we picked up the Navajo Nation radio station. They were also playing great vintage country music; then, after a short pause, a beautiful female voice sang in Navajo. We didn't understand the words, but we knew the melody: "The Star Spangled Banner." Driving Route 66 is always a time to reflect on America, as you look in awe at your natural surroundings. You try to reconcile the social forces—native, Spanish, and Anglo—that created the fragile community that shares this awesome landscape and its pervasive sense of danger mixed with opportunity. What process of reconciliation led a Native American girl to sing this lovely version of an English drinking song, recast as the patriotic anthem of the Europeans who "won the West?" Lyrically, it's not a song of victory. It's a song of survival through the night, under attack from a stronger oppressor. Maybe she was making that connection, or maybe she was making a simple statement of her own patriotism as an American. As the static crept in, the sun was setting in the west far behind us now.

We played our show in New Mexico, then headed south to the land of the Saguaro for a quick show in Arizona before heading partway around the world.

As we pulled out of Phoenix, the temperature on the surface of the car's hood registered 134 degrees. We high-tailed it back across the desert to LAX, where we boarded a plane to New

York, with a connection in Chicago. In New York, we grabbed our own car and drove straight to Boston for an outdoor daytime show. After the show, we left our car with a friend and dashed to Logan airport, where we boarded a transatlantic flight. That one connected in Paris, continuing on to Manchester, England. We were immediately picked up and driven straight to a festival in Southport, which we played under the numbing influence of jet-lag and two days without sleep. The next morning, we caught a ride back to Manchester, where we rented a car and continued all the way down to London for a show at The Green Note. The following morning, it was back to Manchester for a flight to Boston, connecting through Amsterdam. From Boston we located our car and drove down to New York. In fourteen days, we had passed through Phoenix, Los Angeles, Chicago, New York, Boston, Paris, Manchester, London, Amsterdam, and back through Boston to New York!

At the end of some of our UK tours, we would take a jaunt over to the Continent for some vacation time. On one such trip, we stashed our touring gear in a locker at Manchester Airport and caught a flight over to Geneva, Switzerland.

We lodged with Maura's brother Joe, a senior scientist at the CERN nuclear lab, in a converted lumber mill in the tiny French village of Gex. It was near Voltaire's home, at the geographical heart of the Age of Reason. In the morning, I hiked with Joe down into the village square. We bought cheese and fresh fish for, respectively, breakfast and a barbecued dinner on the bank of the millstream that raced down from the Alps. The next day, Maura and I caught a train deeper into France, to Lyon, where we got a ride from our French hostess to a bed and breakfast in Limonest, a few miles north of the old city.

In the morning, we were up early to catch the bus, out on the Charles de Gaulle highway, into the Lyon rail station. As we passed through villages, the bus became crowded and hot. One exasperated mom tried to catch a bit of rest while herding three restless kids. One of her little boys looked at us with curiosity; Maura and I had absent-mindedly spoken to each other in English, drawing his attention. Falling back on the universal language, I pulled my ukulele out of its canvas bag and tuned it up. I'd been doing a bit of busking in the French railway stations over the last few days, so I had a little medley already worked up.

Since my audience, so far, was only the little boy, I started playing softly, with "Ah, Vous Dirai-je, Maman," the melody that kids in the States learn as "Twinkle, Twinkle Little Star." He glanced at his mom to gauge the possible scolding factor, but she was distracted by the wailing baby, so he started to tap his foot. The medley steamed full-speed ahead with "La Vie en Rose" and "The Poor People of Paris." My repertoire of French standards was scant, but it filled the bill when busking for travelers riding the bus on a hot day in June. As the medley segued into Django's "Nuages," and then into an uptempo swing version of "Claire de Lune," it became apparent that all the adults on the bus were tapping their feet, and the long ride down the steep bluff into the old city became a little shorter for all of us.

After a train ride through the Rhone Alps back to Geneva, and an auto trip along the lakeside to a little outdoor café in Nyon, there was time to reflect, as the sunset turned Mont Blanc pink across the lake, on the power of a little uke and some simple melodies to draw people together for a few moments, there at the timeless crossroads of Europe.

Chapter 25: Bright Lights and Hot Rods, and a Manila Envelope

In July of 2014, we traveled up to Syracuse for "Bright Lights," a reunion of bands and fans from Maura's days growing up in the great rock and pop scene there. She put together a band for the occasion, "Maura and the Bright Lights," and we played a set of original songs from Syracuse bands.

Before we buckled down to a bit of rehearsal, we set aside a day to help Maura's dad move into his new digs. He was an author and lifelong professor of American Literature, so it was no surprise that his largest and most precious load of cargo was his book collection. I sat with him as he pulled each volume off the shelf, explaining its importance to me as he turned the pages. Many of those pages sparked memories that went back to the boyhood farm in Minnesota, camping in the north woods, hiking the Appalachian Trail, then military service in Japan, and ultimately to life on campus as a professor. The books meant a lot to him. Their meaning was enlarged for me as he explained their role in the chapters of his own life. The most precious piece of all was a worn manila envelope filled with hand-typed index cards; cards that he had typed out as he first read Thoreau, discovering the path he would follow through life. They were filled with wonder and excitement, typed by a young man finding not only a 19th century mentor, but also finding himself as well. I handled the envelope carefully, like an ancient codex, as we taped the last box shut.

Dinner was on the front porch of the venerable Dinosaur BBQ. The sidewalk was lined with Harleys and B.B King was blasting on the jukebox. The Syracuse Nationals, one of the great hot-rod shows, was happening that same weekend. The street was lined bumper-to-bumper with beautifully restored vintage hot rods: 1950s' Chevys, 1930s' Fords; the swagger of Detroit's glory days.

The following night at 9:00 p.m., Maura and the Bright Lights took the stage at The Lost Horizon, Syracuse's legendary old rock club. The power-pop set was charged with energy, coming not only *from* us, but *at* us as well from the audience. Most of them had come up with Maura through the ranks of the clubs and studios. It was a great night, from the kickoff right through to the encores.

The next morning, as we pulled out of town and headed south on I-81, Maura took something out of her shoulder bag. "Dad said he wanted us to have this." It was the manila envelope containing the index cards; his original Thoreau notes. With our precious cargo on board, we cruised the Catskills effortlessly, buoyed by the energy of music, some good barbecue, and an envelope of inspiration that reached across decades to inspire us.

Chapter 26: A Million More to Go

October 22 of 2014 marked our 20th wedding anniversary. "It was twenty years ago today," but it wasn't Sergeant Pepper who taught The Kennedys to play. It was, indeed, a spontaneous chemistry that happened the very first time we sang together, played together, wrote a song together. That all happened right when we first met, and we both knew that we had found not only a soulmate, but a musical partner for life.

As we celebrated twenty years, Maura and I recalled standing on either side of my dad's hospital bed when he called us over, and said his last words, in a very quiet voice that beckoned us to lean over and listen. He said, "You've gotta help the people." Hopefully, through the simple acts of singing and playing guitar, we found a way to do that.

Epilogue

When I began writing this tale, I considered focusing on certain small moments: the creation of a song, the look on the face of someone in the audience when a lyric seems to speak directly to them, the magic of a great concert. I pinpointed those moments, to be sure, but I knew this couldn't be a microcosmic story. It had to be seen through a wide-angle lens because it covered half a century and traversed a broad landscape: a million miles across North America, Britain, and Ireland.

The passport to all of those moments, whether they were daring adventures or simple exchanges of kindness between strangers, was the guitar. I was playing the guitar when I met Maura, and every one of my journeys had a destination that involved strumming those six strings. Back in my youth, I used to read melodies out of a thick tome entitled "O'Neill's Music of Ireland." It was there that I discovered an old tune called "Peter Kennedy's Fancy." I've always wondered who that Peter Kennedy was, what gigs he played in Ireland, and whether any of his DNA is in my own code. Maybe it was he who whispered in my ear to go down through the darkened bleachers to watch the guitarist on Saint Patrick's Day at the circus so long ago. If so, the final dedication is his.

Pete Kennedy

New York City, 2018

Appendix A: Venues Played

As a guitarist working with great artists, especially Maura, Mary Chapin Carpenter, and Nanci Griffith, I've played in smoky bars and luxurious theaters, including:

Carnegie Hall, New York
The Beacon Theater, New York
The Bottom Line, New York
The City Winery, New York
Joe's Pub, New York
Central Park Summer Stage, New York
Symphony Space, New York
Royal Albert Hall, London, England
Hammersmith Odeon, London, England
Shepherd's Bush Empire, London, England
King's Place, London, England
The Green Note, London, England
Colston Hall, Bristol, England
Manchester Apollo, Manchester, England
Queen's Hall, Edinburgh, Scotland
Brighton Dome, Brighton, England
The Olympia Theater, Dublin, Ireland
Kennedy Center for the Performing Arts, Washington D.C.
Wolf Trap Center for the Performing Arts, Vienna, VA
Sanders Theater, Harvard University, Cambridge, MA
The Cambridge Folk Festival, Cambridge, England
Merriweather Post Pavilion, Columbia, MD
The National Theater, Washington, D.C.
Ford's Theater, Washington, D.C.

The Paramount Theater, Austin, Texas
The Warfield Theater, San Francisco, CA
Old Vic Theater, Chicago, IL
Boston Symphony Hall, Boston, MA
The Newport Folk Festival
The Philadelphia Folk Festival
The Falcon Ridge Festival
The Boston Folk Festival

Appendix B: Awards

~~~~~~

I've also been fortunate enough to win a few music awards from my peers:

1992: Emmy, National Academy of Television Arts and Sciences, Washington D.C. Chapter for "Channel 3" music video.

1992: 15th Annual PhilaFilm Festival Philadelphia, PA for "Channel 3" music video, winner, Gold Award

1992: 25th Annual Worldfest, Houston Texas, Silver Award for "Channel 3" music video

1992: Rosebud Award Nominee, Washington D.C. Mayors Office for the Arts for "Channel 3" music video.

1993: Grammy certificate for participation on Nanci Griffith's "Other Voices, Other Rooms," winner, Best Contemporary Folk Album

1995: National Association of Independent Record Distributors Best Adult Contemporary Album, "River of Fallen Stars"

Washington Area Music Awards:

1985: Best Freelance Musician

1986: Best Roots Rock Instrumentalist

Best Folk Instrumentalist

1987: Best Roots Rock Instrumentalist

Best Folk Instrumentalist

Best Rock/Pop Instrumentalist

Best Rock/Pop Group; Bound for Glory

Best Freelance Musician

Best Pop Recording

1988: Best Folk Instrumentalist
Best Freelance Musician
1989: Best Folk Instrumentalist
Best Freelance Musician
1991: Best Folk Recording
Best Rock Recording
1992: Roots Rock Instrumentalist
Best Rock/Pop Instrumentalist
Artist of the Year
1993: Best Roots Rock Instrumentalist
1994: Best New Artist (The Kennedys)
1995: Best Contemporary Folk Instrumentalist
Best Contemporary Folk Group (The Kennedys)
Best Contemporary Folk Recording (River of Fallen Stars)
Best Contemporary Folk Female Vocalist (Maura Kennedy)
Song of the Year (The Same Old Way)
Artist of the Year (The Kennedys)
1996: Best Contemporary Folk Instrumentalist
Best Contemporary Folk Group (The Kennedys)
Best Contemporary Folk Recording (Life Is Large)
Best Contemporary Folk Female Vocalist (Maura Kennedy)
Best Rock/Pop Instrumentalist
Best Rock/Pop Group (The Kennedys)
Best Roots Rock Group (The Kennedys)
Best Rock/Pop Recording (Life Is Large)
Best Rock/Pop Female Vocalist (Maura Kennedy)
Best Record Design (Life Is Large)
1998: Best Contemporary Folk Group (The Kennedys)
Best Rock/Pop Group (The Kennedys)
Best Contemporary Folk Instrumentalist
Best Contemporary Folk Female Vocalist (Maura Kennedy)
1999: Best Contemporary Folk Group (The Kennedys)
Best Contemporary Folk Instrumentalist
Best Rock/Pop Group (The Kennedys)

Best Rock Pop Instrumentalist
Songwriters of the Year
2000: Best Rock Instrumentalist
Best Rock/Pop Male Vocalist
Best Rock/Pop Female Vocalist (Maura Kennedy)
Best Rock Pop Group (The Kennedys)
Best Rock/Pop Recording (Evolver)
Video of the Year (Free)
2001: Best Contemporary Folk Instrumentalist
Best Rock/Pop Instrumentalist
Best Rock/Pop Recording (Positively Live)
Video of the Year (Nickeltown)

Appendix C: Television Appearances

"That's What Friends are For," live from the Kennedy Center for the Performing Arts, with Elton John, Stevie Wonder, Burt Bacharach, Dionne Warwick, Gladys Knight

"Leonard Bernstein 60th Birthday Gala," Live from The Wolf Trap Center for the Performing Arts, with The National Symphony, conducted by Leonard Bernstein

"A Country Christmas," live from Ford's Theater, with Mary Chapin Carpenter, President George Herbert Walker Bush.

Today, with Mary Chapin Carpenter

The Tonight Show, with Nanci Griffith

Austin City Limits, with Nanci Griffith, Mary Chapin Carpenter

The Terry Wogan Show, BBC-TV, with Nanci Griffith

Later...with Jools Holland, BBC-TV, with Nanci Griffith

"Down on the Farm Festival" with Nanci Griffith, Halden, Norway, televised on Norwegian TV

Pebble Mill, BBC-TV, with Nanci Griffith

"The Cambridge Folk Festival 2012," BBC-TV, with Nanci Griffith

Appendix D: *Discography*

Pete Kennedy Solo Albums (produced by Pete Kennedy unless otherwise noted):

Rhythm Ranch (1985 Rosewood Records; 1986 Rooster Records LP & cassette)

Sunburst (1985 Rosewood Records; 1986 Rooster Records, LP & cassette)

Bound For Glory (1986 Rosewood Records, LP & cassette)

19 in Vietnam (single only; 1987 Rosewood Records)

Distant Thunder (1988 Potomac Disc, cassette only)

Live at the Birchmere (1989 no label, cassette only)

Highway 10 (1990 Pete Kennedy Music, CD & cassette)

Channel 3 (1992 Third Floor Records, CD & cassette)

Shearwater (1992 Third Floor Records, 1993 Guitar Recordings CD & cassette)

Fingers On Fire: Tom Principato and Pete Kennedy (2002 Powerhouse Records and produced by Tom Principato)

Guitarslinger (2008 The Kennedys, LLC)

Tone, Twang, and Taste (2014 The Kennedys, LLC)

Heart Of Gotham (2015 The Kennedys, LLC)

The Kennedys (produced by Pete Kennedy or co-produced with Maura Kennedy):

River of Fallen Stars (1995 Green Linnet; 2003 Varese Sarabande Records)

Life Is Large (1996 Green Linnet; 2003 Varese Sarabande Records)

Angel Fire (1998 Rounder/Philo)

Evolver (2000 Rounder/Zoe)

Positively Live! (2001 Jiffyjam)

Get It Right (2002 Jiffyjam)

Stand (2003 KOCH; The Kennedys, LLC)

Half a Million Miles (2005 Appleseed Recordings)

Songs of the Open Road (2006 Appleseed Recordings)

Better Dreams (2008 Appleseed Recordings)

Retrospective (2012 The Kennedys, LLC)

Closer Than You Know (2012 The Kennedys, LLC)

Dance a Little Closer (2014 The Kennedys, LLC)

West (2015 The Kennedys, LLC)

Safe Until Tomorrow (2018 The Kennedys, LLC)

The Kennedys' Side Projects (co-produced with Maura Kenendy):

The Strangelings—The Nuah Suite live DVD (2006)

The Stringbusters—Rhapsody in Uke (2007 The Kennedys, LLC)

The Strangelings—Season of the Witch (2007 The Kennedys, LLC)

Pete Kennedy Session Work:

Pete Kennedy played on a number of recordings by ather artists. A selection follows:

Eric Andersen, *The Street Was Always There*

Mike Auldridge, *Eight String Swing*

Bedsit Poets, *February Kisses*

Delia Bell and Bill Grant, *A Few Dollars More* (uncredited)

Mary Chapin Carpenter, *The Best Of Mountain Stage, Volume 3*

Hazel Dickens, Carol Elizabeth Jones & Ginny Hawke, *Heart of a Singer*

Eddie From Ohio, *Actually Not*

Edward Rogers, *Porcelain* and others

Jonathan Edwards, *Man in the Moon*

Cathy Fink & Marcy Marxer, *Help Yourself* and others

Gary Frenay, *Jigsaw People*

Nanci Griffith, *Other Voices, Other Rooms* and others

Si Kahn, *I'll Be There: Songs for Jobs with Justice*

Maura Kennedy, *Parade Of Echoes & Villanelle*

John McCutcheon, *Gonna Rise Again* and twenty others

Patsy Montana, *The Cowboy's Sweetheart*

The Nields, *If You Lived Here You'd Be Home Now*

Tom Paxton, *Your Shoes, My Shoes* and others

Sally Rogers, *Generations*

Rosslyn Mountain Boys, *Lone Outsider*

The Smith Sisters, *Roadrunner*

…and a many more with independent artists.

Pete Kennedy Also Produced:

Trouble in the Fields: An Artists' Tribute to Nanci Griffith (2012 Paradiddle Records)

Intersection—Nanci Griffith (2012 Hell No Records co-produced with Maura Kennedy)

…and a variety of independent releases.

Index

~~~~~~

Credits

Publisher/Editorial Director: Michael Roney

Art Director: Sarah M. Clarehart

Copyeditor: Caroline Berry

Proofreader: Katharine Dvorak

Index: Maura Kennedy

Life

HIGHPOINT